STILL DOING
THE
IMPOSSIBLE

When You See the Invisible, You Can Do the Impossible

ORAL ROBERTS

Destiny Image® Publishers, Inc.
P.O. Box 310
Shippensburg, PA 17257-0310

"Speaking to the Purposes of God for This
Generation and for the Generations to Come"

ISBN 0-7684-2060-1

For Worldwide Distribution
Printed in the U.S.A.

This book and all other Destiny Image, Revival Press, MercyPlace, Fresh Bread, Destiny Image Fiction, and Treasure House books are available at Christian bookstores and distributors worldwide.

For a U.S. bookstore nearest you, call **1-800-722-6774**.
For more information on foreign distributors, call **717-532-3040**.
Or reach us on the Internet:

www.destinyimage.com

CONTENTS

INTRODUCTION

Some people might look at the more than half century of my ministry and say, "He's an old preacher. How can he advise me?" Others will say, "He's not a preacher who is old, but one who obeys God, is experienced in the things I face in my life, and can help answer questions facing me."

To say that my body is no longer young, and growing older by the year, is true—but *the whole story* includes:

- the vibrancy of the Spirit within me,

- a mind constantly renewed through the prayer language of the Spirit and interpretation back to my mind,

- the miracle of Seed-Faith dominating my way of giving and receiving.

All of these hold back the aging process and renew my strength like the eagle's. (See Isaiah 40:31.) I can travel coast-to-coast and border-to-border with a heavy anointing, preaching with the fire of the Lord in my spirit and feeling the miraculous power of God in my teaching, preaching, and healing ministry, as well as in my calling as an author and educator.

What I say in this book is as real as God is real and as fresh as the morning dew. The advice I give in this book is not mere book knowledge, although I am a student of both the spiritual and secular worlds. I have been where you are but have refused to sit there while I die. (See Second Kings 7:3.) I've risen up and struck a blow for deliverance. I've sat where you sit; I've felt what you feel; I've seen the invisible and *done* the impossible.

That's what I want to challenge you to do! *Obey God, see the invisible, and do the impossible.*

Before Moses could undertake the impossible task of delivering the children of Israel from Egyptian bondage, it is said, he saw the invisible! "By faith he forsook Egypt, not fearing the wrath of the king: for he endured, as seeing Him who is invisible" (Heb. 11:27).

By faith he was able to see Him (Jesus) who is invisible to the naked eye. Seeing Him with his spirit changed Moses' entire focus from a stuttering, faltering, and unbelieving man to an extraordinary talking, firm, believing, and anointed man who literally did the impossible both in Egypt and all the way to the Promised Land.

He saw the invisible first,
    then he was able to do the impossible.

I saw the invisible when the doctors had just told my parents death was near for me. My father, mother, and the nurse knelt by my bed to pray a desperate prayer for me to accept Christ. My father said, "Son, I cannot stand to see you die and lose your soul."

As they prayed I paid little attention. I had heard them pray all my life, with no effect on me.

When my mother and the nurse finished praying and sat back up in their chairs, my father kept praying. Kneeling at the

6

foot of my bed, and with tears streaming down his face, he raised up on his knees and called on God for his son to be saved. He seemed completely lost in his prayer.

Suddenly, looking across my bed, I "saw" my father's face fade and the countenance of Jesus appear in its place.

In terms of time it was like a lightning experience, but it was clear and unmistakable. I actually saw Him—whether with my human eyes or inner vision, I do not know. In that moment, I saw the invisible and it broke me up. I, who had never remembered praying or desiring God, was shaken to the roots of my soul.

In the flash of a second I heard myself crying out in a loud voice, "Save me, Jesus, save me." During the next minute or two my sins flooded up within me; I felt and saw them, and I knew for the first time that I was a sinner. I cried out my repentance and remember saying, "Jesus, I'll even preach for You if You'll save my soul."

At that moment the irresistible power of Jesus' presence and unspeakable joy filled my being. Nothing like this had ever happened to me before. In seeing the invisible, my life opened and I knew I could do the impossible. Soon I was miraculously healed (I tell this story in Chapter 1), heard Jesus' call on my life, specifically telling me what I was to accomplish for Him (all of it impossible by man's view), and I entered a new life and world.

Less than 20 years later God's command for me to build a major university, founded on His authority and the Holy Spirit, became a reality. I had to see the invisible before I could do the impossible. Otherwise, I would not have been able to see the land and buildings, the students and faculty, or the accreditation. They would have seemed totally impossible.

I cannot overemphasize what I believe to be absolutely necessary for anyone receiving Christ—that is to have *some form* of seeing the invisible. It does not have to be as I saw, or as Moses saw, but each in his own way. I'm totally convinced after dealing with multitudes of people—in their sins and sickness, and seeing great numbers of them saved and healed— that each of them, in some way real to them, saw the invisible and saw themselves doing the impossible.

The Bible says understanding is gained from the Word of God and life's experiences. (See Proverbs 3:13.) At age 84, I have had much of both. It is from the understanding God has allowed me to gain that I share with you my advice and my life—the mistakes, triumphs, and revelations.

I have attempted to write the kind of book I would have given anything to find when I began to obey God's call on my life.

I invite you to take from this book every single thought that *fits where you are* as if Jesus Himself is talking to you. For that simple reason, I only say what I've experienced in Him and say only what He has told me to say. Early in my ministry, my five-foot-tall mama told me, "Oral, obey God and stay small in your own eyes."

It's my greatest desire that through this book, God will move so mightily on you that you will not only see the invisible, but also begin to do the impossible He has called you to do!

Part One

SEEING THE INVISIBLE

1

How God Taught Me to See the Invisible and Do the Impossible

There were people who said...

- "Oral Roberts will never be a preacher. In fact, he can't even talk without stuttering."

- "Oral Roberts will never amount to much because his family is so poor."

- "His healing ministry will last only two months because nobody is doing what he is doing in ministry."

- "The concept of Seed-Faith is just a gimmick and won't work."

- "Oral Roberts University will never be built because Oral Roberts doesn't know how to build a university."

Many people said many things about Oral Roberts, but what mattered was what God said. Isaiah 55:9 says that His thoughts are higher than our thoughts. So I decided to believe

God's thoughts about me and go for something higher than what others had planned for me. The results have been miraculous!

If you think you aren't going to make it in what God has called you to do in your life,
> or if you feel discouraged because all you can see is what look like failures,
>> or if you are hungry to know how to succeed for God—
then stay glued to what I'm sharing with you in this book, reread it at least once a year, and put into practice its principles. I believe you *will* be raised into success by almighty God.

The following story illustrates what it takes to be successful.

There was once a young man (I'll call him Jim) who wanted to be a success, but he didn't know how. Jim knew of an older man in the city (Mr. Smith), who was the most influential, the wealthiest, and the most successful; and he desperately wanted to meet the older gentleman.

One day, arriving at his favorite fishing spot, Jim saw Mr. Smith fishing nearby.

So he walked up to him and said, "Mr. Smith, my name is Jim. Can I fish by you?"

Mr. Smith answered, "Well, son, sit right down here and be my guest."

After a while Jim said, "Sir, I've wanted to be successful all my life, and you're the only successful man I've ever met. Would you tell me how to be a success?"

The older man said, "Yes. Stand on your feet." He promptly shoved Jim into the water, got him by the hair of the head, and plunged him under.

Pretty soon Mr. Smith jerked Jim's head up as the boy struggled to get his breath. Suddenly he shoved Jim's head under the water again, pulled him up, and watched as he was still trying to breathe.

The third time Mr. Smith shoved Jim under and kept him under—until he knew he'd better get the boy up or he'd drown. As Jim came up, he was gasping hard for breath. Mr. Smith finally said to him, "Son, do you know how badly you wanted that last breath? When you want to be a success like you wanted that last breath, you *will be* a success."

Over the past 37 years of Oral Roberts University's existence, many ministers and businesspeople have come to 7777 South Lewis in Tulsa, Oklahoma, taken a room in the hotel across the street, and stood at the window where they could see the whole campus. As they walked the grounds and saw the 22 major buildings, including the 200-foot-high Prayer Tower, they said in themselves, "If God can do this through one man, He can enable me to build what I need and to expand my ministry or in my profession to fulfill my destiny." These people were seeing what was once invisible, and their faith was stirred to do the impossible. They saw the result of obedience that comes from faith.

I'm no different from you. I am just as human as you are. Through obedience you can see miraculous results in your life too.

God Pours Out Ideas

As you read about my life's events and what I have learned from God, you will receive two basic things. First, you will capture *ideas*. We operate from the ideas that God gives us. I call it ICI—ideas, concepts, and insights.

Malachi 3:10 says, "Bring ye all the tithes into the storehouse, that there may be meat in Mine house, and prove Me now herewith, saith the Lord of hosts, if I will not open you the windows of heaven, and pour you out a blessing, that there shall not be room enough to receive it." God was talking about multiplying our tithes—as seed sown—back to us. He was talking about *ideas*, *concepts*, and *insights*. Everything begins with an idea. God had an idea to create the world. He had an idea to create man. He had an idea to send Jesus. Everybody does what they do with an idea.

God begins by pouring an idea out of Heaven. Then it becomes a concept. Once the concept becomes a way of life, God gives you insight or wisdom in how to apply the idea. As a consistent tither who expects miracle harvests from my seed sown (see 1 Cor. 3:7; Gal. 6:7-9), ICI has been at the center of my life and ministry.

The second thing you will receive from this book is that you will learn a *method*, a method for every idea. I have lived by this statement: *I am married to principles, but I am not married to methods.* I never change a principle in which I believe, but whatever method God calls me to use to accomplish the principle, I do. Do not be married to particular methods. Principles are absolutes but methods are variables. God may use different methods to fulfill His absolute principles through your life.

That is one reason I was able to reach millions of people with the healing ministry. I did not let conventional methods stop me. When the experts told me that cameras couldn't be brought into the big tent crusades, we did it anyway. Millions of people at home saw the miraculous healings right there on their television sets. Their faith was stirred to the point that they could believe for a great healing miracle. In 1954 I was the first to use that method; as a result, millions of hurting people grew in faith.

I was standing on the principle that divine healing is for every man, woman, boy, and girl! We had to find a way to get healing to them. We did it through a God-given idea, an idea I wrestled with by my faith until it became a "knowing" in my heart. The impossible, at that time when healing was virtually unknown in America, even in the churches, could be done; and I was a God-called man to release my faith and do it!

One thing about an idea from God—there is a special time to do it. You must gather all your faith, release it to God, and start doing it.

As we go on this journey to success through obedience, let faith grab hold of your spirit to *see the invisible and do the impossible.*

IMPORTANT POINTS

1. Listen to God's thoughts for your life.

2. You've got to want God's success badly enough.

3. Be open to ICI—Ideas, Concepts, and Insights—from God.

4. Be married to principles but not to methods.

5. Know you have the faith to do all God has planned for you to do.

2

HOW I LEARNED NOT TO MISS THE *KEY ISSUE*!

My story is a testimony to the power and drama of what God can do through the life of someone who is obedient—who is willing to look squarely at the invisible and to attempt the impossible.

What I'm about to share with you is about people—people like you and me who are born with an inclination to go a certain way in life. Throughout our lives that inclination grows stronger and stronger to be a particular kind of person, good or bad.

Everybody is different, yet he or she has to fit into the human race and human society to become a success. Many people do not find a fit that satisfies them or those around them. They fail to find the *key issue*, the bottom line, of what it takes to fulfill what they desire and hunger to be and to do.

In many ways the earth is a junk pile upon which are heaped human beings who fail to find their place and who are unfulfilled and disillusioned. That does not have to be. We need only to begin to understand and believe that there is a higher Power, who is God, and that He is interested in and concerned about us. When we look toward the invisible by turning ourselves toward the Supreme Being, we will find the impossible much easier than we thought.

Just in time, I came to realize in my own life

- that God desires each of us to awaken to His awareness,

- that He alone can show us how to walk through the pitfalls of life,

- that He knew us before we were born and had planned our lives and careers,

- that by listening we would find our place, and it would be the greatest fit possible.

I learned that God has a specific life and calling—a specific purpose—He wants each of us to know and follow in every area of our lives.

I thought I knew the way my life was to be and to go. Mine was like the song Frank Sinatra sang, "I Did It My Way." I listened to no one but myself, and I believed God had little or nothing to do with my life.

Well, I was wrong. Dead wrong. I had missed the central point of life—the *key issue*. I did not learn that God had "the way" for me to know what I was to become until just hours before it seemed too late.

I was born the fifth and last child of my parents. My mother vowed to God that if her last child would be a son (with black hair and blue eyes—the other children were brown-eyed), he would preach the gospel, pray for the sick, and do other impossible things for God.

Although I was born a preacher's kid (a PK), becoming a preacher was a million miles from my mind. Being reared in the church, I had had enough of religion. It held no interest for me.

I Wanted to Do It My Way!

With a vengeance I was pursuing an entirely different plan. I left home as a teenager to make my own way, to have freedom from my parents' constant urgings for me to let God rule my life.

In spite of the fact that I was born a stutterer, I knew exactly what I wanted to be: a lawyer like my grandfather Amos Pleasant Roberts, who was a frontier judge in Oklahoma while it was still Indian territory. As foolish as it sounds, someday I wanted to be governor of my home state, Oklahoma. I was determined that nobody and nothing would keep me from reaching those goals.

Then I received the shock of my life. I discovered there were forces in life too strong for me. As a high school sophomore, while playing in a district basketball championship, I fell unconscious to the floor. Tuberculosis, the disease so prevalent in my little Cherokee mother's people, had settled in my lungs. When I came to and was examined and pronounced to be in the last stages of this horrible disease, I felt I might as well be dead already, for in 1935 there was no medical cure for this infectious disease.

My mother's father and her two older sisters had died with it; I believed I would be the next.

The driving force I had felt to go "my way" died within me. I realized for the first time that whether it's an incurable disease or some other hindering cause, something out there was evil. It was there to take me out before I even had a real chance in life.

I felt death pulling at me time and time again in my terrible suffering and pain. Grieving over my plight, night after night my mother whispered in my ear, "Oral, God is not going to let the devil kill you. You were born to preach the gospel, as your father has done, and someday pray for the sick, as I've done."

All this sounded so far away, so strange. I lay five months hovering between life and death. I could feel nothing inside me responding to God until my sister, Jewel, came to my bedside and said seven words that changed my life forever: "Oral, God is going to heal you."

A loving God had heard both my parents' prayers and sought to honor them. My conversion now came quickly, for my heart had been touched by a power I had not personally known.

Jewel's words were prophetic. Elmer, my oldest brother—now married with a family, our ages separated by 14 years—came one day with news that took my breath away. His wife, Ora, a devout believer, had been attending a revival in my hometown, Ada, where an evangelist, George C. Moncey, had prayer for the sick as part of his ministry.

"Get up, Oral," Elmer said. "I've come to take you to this revival. God is going to heal you."

Although not a Christian, Elmer, like the rest of us, had been influenced by the faith of our mother, Claudius Priscilla Roberts, who was often called by neighbors to come and pray when a loved one had been given up by the doctors.

On the way to the revival, lying in the backseat of the car, I had my first personal encounter with God.

I heard the voice of God!

"Son, I am going to heal you, and you are to take My healing power to your generation."

I can't explain it and don't attempt to, because it was beyond anything I had ever experienced. It was His voice:

clear,

distinct,

unmistakable.

As I pondered what I had heard, He spoke again, "*You are to build Me a university. Build it on My authority and on the Holy Spirit.*" I knew without the shadow of a doubt that I had heard God's voice.

By now I felt I was living in two worlds. On the one hand, I was sick unto death. On the other, I was being carried for healing prayer. I had gone from my normal weight of 165 pounds on my six-foot-one-and-a-half-inch frame down to 120 pounds of, skin and bones.

When we made it to the service, the minister anointed me with oil and prayed a prayer, the words of which seemed to penetrate every fiber of my being: "You foul, tormenting disease, I command you in the name of Jesus Christ of Nazareth, you come out of this young man. Loose him and let him go free!"

I felt healing instantly in both my lungs and in my speech, but it took months to recover my strength and to realize I was actually free from a stuttering tongue and that I was *called to preach the gospel*.

IMPORTANT POINTS

1. God has a specific calling and plan—a higher purpose— for your life.

2. Don't miss the key issue God is trying to show you concerning His plan for you. Concentrate on finding the key issue, the bottom line, for which way your life is to go.

3. One touch from God can change the entire direction of your life. One glimpse of the invisible can break you up inside and cause you to start your life in the right direction: God's.

4. Never give up on yourself.

3

HOW I DISCOVERED
WHERE AND HOW I FIT

I was healed in an era when healing by faith was seldom preached. The very idea that it was God's will to heal was something that happened two thousand years ago, not in our time. But there I was, a living example of God's provision and will to heal the sick and hurting. People flocked to hear my little sermons and my glowing healing testimony.

There was little doubt that I had had a genuine, medically tested healing from an incurable disease. The stuttering son of Reverend E. M. Roberts people had known during my growing-up years could actually talk with a freed-up tongue.

More calls came for me to speak than I could fill. I had become a wonder of God to myself and to increasing numbers of people and churches.

I knew that I had to finish high school, go to college, and prepare myself to preach the gospel just as I had planned to prepare to become a lawyer.

I began the process of preaching little sermons, giving my testimony, and working on my education.

Through God's sovereign plan (explained in more detail in Chapter 10), I met Evelyn Lutman, a young schoolteacher and strong believer. We fell in love deeply at age 21 with a knowing that we were made for each other. She was eager to assist me in getting my education. Eventually Evelyn became my wife and mother of the four children—Rebecca, Ronnie, Richard, and Roberta—with whom we were blessed.

In those first years of my new ministry, I carried an average of 70 theological books in the trunk of my car as I traveled. I was a student by nature, purpose, and determination.

Time moved swiftly into years. Twelve years later, with all I had done—preaching, going to universities, studying theology from books—*I still had not found my place in ministry*. Where did I fit?

I did not doubt my calling.

I simply could not find my place in God.

I was a pastor of small churches at times. At other times I was an evangelist, and at all times a student. I never stopped learning during those first 12 years. After finding my place in ministry, I actually increased my studies and obtained college and seminary degrees.

Don't misunderstand me. I had "devoured" the Bible. In those first 12 years of trying to find my place in God, I had read the New Testament through consecutively over a hundred times, and the entire Bible dozens of times. How did I find time to do it? The answer is that you do what you want and will to do. I wanted, yearned, and willed to learn what God had said in His Word, and particularly how it spoke to me.

God Is a Talking God!

He had spoken to me in the backseat of my brother's car. And once I was totally sure I had heard God's words to me, I never doubted them. That they have come to pass is the proof that He did speak into my spirit.

I hear preachers and other believers frequently say God said such and such to them. I always look for the evidence, the results.

The Lord said, "Behold, I stand at the door, and knock: if any man hear My voice, and open the door, I will come in to him, and will sup with him, and he with Me" (Rev. 3:20). To me that means His voice is speaking. He has a message of great purpose for each of us. However, He put the word *if* in there, implying we have to be *listening at all times*, that we need to have a *listening ear*.

God is a talking God. We are a talking people. Through His Son Jesus, He sits where we sit. He feels what we feel. He wants to converse with us, to have communion (not the Lord's Supper only), and to have a most familiar relationship together.

The way He spoke to me in the beginning, and over 20 times since, has led me to this decision:

I will never attempt anything in His name
unless I hear it first from Him
in a way I cannot mistake.

Being human and having so many adversaries, I find it difficult enough to do anything for God—even when we clearly hear inside us and know His spoken word is backed up by His written Word. To attempt God's work on what we merely conjure up ourselves is the height of foolishness, and often devastating.

25

In my struggle to find my place in God, I drew the line, as the apostle Paul did. I did not confer with flesh and blood to attempt something important in God's name (see Gal. 1:16). After Paul's powerful conversion, healing, and calling, before he met with any of the other apostles, he went off alone for three solid years to get his bearings, to really find his place in God.

Once I knew my God-ordained place, I obeyed God with everything in me, against all odds and no matter the cost in misunderstanding, persecution, ostracism, and just plain hard work in staying the course. Knowing my place in God became a driving force, a consuming passion, which I continue to feel to this day. There is nothing like it in the world.

Finding Your Place in God

In sharing with ministers and other business and career people over the years, I have heard the same questions from many of them: "How can I succeed like so-and-so? Why can't I do what they're doing?"

I usually answer with a line of questions rather than trying to judge them.

"Where in the Bible does God ask you to do the work someone else is doing? *Have you found your place in God?* If not, why not? If you have, why don't you look more closely at what God has called you to do, and determine if it is unique to you? Your highest honor is to do what He's called you to do, not to be the clone of another."

In my view, based on long experience and on knowing the core principles of the Word of God, God gets no glory out of us all being just alike. Each of us is unique and irreplaceable.

You may see the way a person is doing a powerful work, on television or in some other noteworthy field. But there is no possible way for you to successfully do the same thing without first hearing God speak into your spirit the clear word, the clear outline on how and when to do it, then receiving the clear open door to do it.

When I say God speaks into your spirit, I am referring to your hearing His voice and lining it up with the Bible, the Word of God itself; of seeing the invisible; and feeling a knowing of faith inside yourself that you can *do* the impossible.

You'll know you have found your place in God when you fit like a hand in a glove, when as a minister you become totally focused on spreading the gospel, which is the power of God (see Rom. 1:16), or when, in another career, you are focused enough that you have a "knowing" you are in God's will.

Knowing your place in God doesn't happen in one day. It requires time, experience, endurance, obedience, and staying the course. But once you know it, never give it up.

To me, there's just no other way. God is our Source, and that's His way.

IMPORTANT POINTS

1. Face up to God's command and provision for finding your place in Him. You do not have to settle for second or third best. Double your efforts that you have been putting into your ministry, your career, and your life. With God it is never too late. But you have to act when He speaks. As you begin, as I did, to see the invisible, follow it. Remember, "Things which are seen were not made of things which do appear" (Heb. 11:3b).

2. To find your place in God: Become absolutely committed to finding it, and you will find yourself getting into it as gracefully as an eagle settles into her nest.

4

HOW I BECAME SURE OF MY CALL, MY PURPOSE IN LIFE

n Romans 10:13-15, God states His way for a believer to become a preacher.

For whosoever shall call upon the name of the Lord shall be saved. How then shall they call on Him in whom they have not believed? and how shall they believe in Him of whom they have not heard? and how shall they hear without a preacher? and how shall they preach, except they be sent? as it is written, How beautiful are the feet of them that preach the gospel of peace, and bring glad tidings of good things!

The only way any of us can have a divine right to minister and preach the gospel, is *to be sent*—to receive a direct, personal call from the Lord Himself. Why? Without it you will fail yourself and God's purposes.

As far as the ministry is concerned, the call can't be handed down to us by family, friends, or the church itself. We must receive *revelation knowledge* from God that is clear and unmistakable. Then we are in a position to obey or disobey—no middle ground, no way to compromise. The call resonates in every part of our being.

I remember how I shivered and shook inside myself when, immediately after I was converted, God's call to preach came into my consciousness. Through an incredible revelation to my spirit, I heard His call in every cell of my body, every organ of my physical being, every part of my mind, my inner man.

It was as irresistible as breathing in and out, and as drinking water and eating food were to my body. It was as real as if Jesus were speaking directly to me, "Son, I am calling you to preach My gospel."

In a real sense, from God's standpoint, you receive a call to your career even if it's not for the ministry. As for me, I began to see the invisible, the possibility that someday I could do the impossible.

I know many ministers have told me their call was not that personal, clear, decisive. Some have said the realization that they were to preach the gospel came months, even years later.

Others have told me they never had an inner sense God was personally calling them to preach His gospel. They simply thought it was a good thing. They went to seminary and learned knowledge of the Bible and of the world, including history of the Bible days and the events told by Bible writers. They studied psychology and sociology. Then they were convinced they could *learn* to fit their lives into some denomination as a pastor or teacher.

I respect anyone who seeks to do good in this manner. But it's not for me, nor for anyone thinking of entering the ministry of a personal God, who knew you while you were in your mother's womb, who knows the way you're made, who knows your name and address.

Why do I say that? I say it...

- because of my understanding of the Word of God and of the plan of salvation He has given,

- from my very close observation of all types of ministers,

- and from my own experience of the profound call I received.

I see a very serious problem in our society, our world, because of people going into the ministry—or into some other career—without first having received a call from God.

There is a disastrous watering down of the preaching of the gospel which is not based solely on the Word of God and revelation knowledge by the Holy Spirit. We have more preaching and teaching on less of the gospel—sometimes on completely no gospel at all. This leaves man more religious than spiritual. If one is not a minister but in another career, he may become more secular than spiritual. Both secular and spiritual aspects are planned to go hand in hand.

In contrast, there is an all-out way of preaching the gospel based solely on the unchanging Word of the living God, in which it becomes the "power of God unto salvation" (Rom. 1:16). The goal is not a mere religious profession, with no transforming power of God to take people from darkness to light (see Acts 26:18). This preaching delivers a message that keeps people from going in the wide gate and the roadway that lead to hell, and instead to enter in the straight gate and nar-row way that lead to eternal life (see Mt. 7:13-14).

The first way of preaching lacks the anointing that Jesus said He had when He preached the gospel:

31

The Spirit of the Lord is upon Me, because He hath anointed Me to preach the gospel to the poor; He hath sent Me to heal the brokenhearted, to preach deliverance to the captives, and recovering of sight to the blind, to set at liberty them that are bruised, to preach the acceptable year of the Lord (Luke 4:18-19).

A man or woman who professes to be a preacher may be a good person. But if that preacher is not *anointed* as Jesus was, or does not preach as Jesus did, there is a problem. That man or woman either is not called or doesn't know the way God calls His ministers.

Upon hearing me talk about this, one young preacher confirmed to me that he had not received a *definite* call. He had entered the ministry because he was altruistic, wanting to make the best of his life. He asked me, "How can I know God is truly calling me?" Here is what I told him:

First, take your concordance and search the Bible for every instance where God selected a man or woman to carry His Word and to be His spokesperson. I believe you'll find in every case that the person received a call.

Next, go to the four Gospels and study how each apostle was selected. Did Jesus call each of them?

Third, thoroughly study the Book of Acts. Look at the lives of those who were not apostles like the Twelve were; those who later became apostles (like Saul of Tarsus, later called Paul), including Barnabas, Silas, Timothy, Titus, Aquila and Priscilla; and the women referred to by Paul in Romans 16. Read that whole chapter over and over.

I told him I could give him many other references in every book in the Bible, to show that God apparently never asked or commanded anyone to do His special work without a definite and unmistakable call spoken directly to the individual.

I asked him whether he had seen the invisible—the *key issue* to doing the impossible.

My advice to anyone concerning this is, regardless of your age, or your station as a preacher/teacher of the gospel—or in some other area—take time off, seek God, study His Word and those whom He called. Ask Him to reveal Himself to you. Believe He will do it. He is more concerned than you are that *if* you preach, you are preaching His gospel and that you are called. The only possibility of your success in preaching or any area is in knowing He called you to do it.

You will never regret taking the time to know God's call! Neither will the people who hear your message or receive your service.

The Call Sets You Apart

This was brought home to me 12 years after I had received the call from God. I was pastoring a church during that time and attending a church-related university. Sitting in a sociology class, I heard the professor say, "It is a scientific impossibility for God to have made a woman out of a man's rib." He went on to disparage the creation of man and woman as given in Genesis 1–2.

I was not a member of that denomination but had been given the privilege of attending that school. I was stunned. To my surprise, the other students of that old-line historic church-related school neither asked the professor any questions nor made any comments.

I stood, held up my hand, and asked to be excused. The professor nodded.

As I went toward my car, God clearly spoke these words to me,

"Son, don't be like other men. Don't be like other preachers. Don't be like any denomination. Be like Jesus, and heal the people as He did."

When God told me not to be like others, I was astonished. He struck a blow at the very mistake I had been making. I was trying to mold my ministry after those preachers/teachers I admired, actually becoming not a voice but an *echo*. (I will say more about this in Chapter 5.)

I had also sought with my whole attitude to become like others in my denomination, and I looked quite a lot to other denominations, such as the one whose university I was attending, for role models.

When He said, "Don't be like other men," my first thoughts were, *If I become virtually totally different from my fellowman, who would I be? What would I look like? How would I be perceived? Did it mean I was to act superior to others?*

I took this hard.

Then I thought of the rest of what God had said. "You be like Jesus and heal the people as He did." I had studied Jesus' life and ministry. I remembered that learned men had been sent to catch Him in His words. After their encounter with Him, they were so impressed they reported back to their leaders that no man ever spoke like this man (see Jn. 7:46).

The light began to dawn inside me. Jesus was different. His apostles and followers in the early Church were different.

They acted differently.

They spoke differently.

They prayed differently.

They preached differently.

They taught differently.

They healed differently.

They saw the world differently.

They saw themselves differently.

I remembered the scribes, Pharisees, and the whole body of ecclesiastical leaders reacting to the ministry of the apostles and early Church leaders after the healing of the lame man at the temple's gate Beautiful in Jerusalem:

Be it known unto you all, and to all the people of Israel, that by the name of Jesus Christ of Nazareth, whom ye crucified, whom God raised from the dead, even by Him doth this man stand here before you whole. This is the stone which was set at nought of you builders, which is become the head of the corner. Neither is there salvation in any other: for there is none other name under heaven given among men, whereby we must be saved. Now when they saw the boldness of Peter and John, and perceived that they were unlearned and ignorant men, they marvelled; and they took knowledge of them, that they had been with Jesus. And beholding the man which was healed standing with them, they could say nothing against it.

But when they had commanded them to go aside out of the council, they conferred among themselves, saying, What shall we do to these men? for that indeed a notable miracle hath been done by them is manifest to all them that dwell in Jerusalem; and we cannot deny it. But that it spread no further among the people, let us straitly threaten them, that they speak henceforth to no man in this name. And they called them, and commanded them not to speak at all nor teach in the name of Jesus. But Peter and John answered and said unto them, Whether it be right in the sight of God to hearken unto you more than unto God, judge ye. For we cannot but speak the things which we have seen and heard (Acts 4:10-20).

It blew me away! They were not like other men, not like other religious leaders. I was. They were like Jesus and healed the people as He did! I was not and did not.

It was the awakening of my life and ministry from the rut of imitation I had allowed myself to fall into, when after my conversion God had given me His unmistakable *call* to preach His gospel, to take His healing power to my generation, and someday to build Him a university.

After I'm gone, others will have to judge how well I've obeyed God's command not to be an echo but to be a voice like Jesus. As far as my own conviction is concerned, I've tried to be that voice with every fiber of my being, regardless of the cost. I have no regrets. I only wish I could have done it better.

Today as I near the finish line, I pour out my last ounce of spiritual, mental, and physical strength. I want to be able to say with Paul, "I have fought a good fight, I have finished my course, I have kept the faith" (2 Tim. 4:7).

IMPORTANT POINTS

1. Know that you know God has truly called you to minister or to have a special career in some other field.

2. Stay out of the rut of imitation. Be what God has called you to be.

3. Get alone with God, and stay alone as long as necessary in seeking Him concerning your calling.

4. Never doubt that He is a talking God, you are a talking person, and He desires to talk to you personally—either audibly, by a deep impression, or by His Word.

5. Remember, it can be done, and you can know the clear path God has laid out for you.

5

HOW I LEARNED
TO BECOME AN ORIGINAL!

learned that God has called each of us to be an original instead of being made out of *man's mold*!

When I first launched into preaching the gospel, I made a serious mistake. As I mentioned earlier, I had become an *echo* rather than a *voice*. Why? I thought that to successfully reach people with the gospel, I had to be like other ministers, watching and copying their style.

As a young preacher, I let my ambition to get ahead cause me to push too fast. I secured other preachers' sermon outlines and made them too much a part of my own instead of digging deeper into the Scriptures for the type of sermons God would anoint me to preach and teach.

I have a vivid memory of how all this began to change, how I approached my study of the Bible in a different way. I developed these *methods* of study not only to prepare my messages but also to truly become an original.

First, I constantly read the Bible through three or four times a year, studying its history and core teachings, and the *key issue* of God's purpose in restoring mankind to Himself. As a serious Bible student, I thirsted to get the whole view of the times in which God's Word had been written and the reason it had been written. I was excited to find that it all correlates into a cohesive whole. The Bible was written by inspired writers, most of whom lived in different eras, didn't know each other, or didn't know what others had written under the inspiration of the Holy Spirit.

Because I had dug deep into God's Word, when I stood up to preach and teach it, I felt I was on a *firm foundation* that was unshakable and workable both in our daily lives and in eternity. My study helped me develop a confidence when I ministered. I knew better how to apply my messages to the direct, personal needs of people, who were at heart the same in every generation.

I learned from the core teaching in the Bible that when I was dealing with one person with the gospel, I was dealing with all people.

The second way I studied the Bible was to look at events that brought major changes through the continuous revelation of God's truth. For example, when I studied the Old Testament (covenant), I saw how it ended with the Book of Malachi, followed by four hundred so-called silent years during which there was no prophet. All things were in preparation for the birth of the promised Messiah. Then God raised up a man to pave the way: John the Baptist.

Among the exciting things that stand out to me about John's life was his preparing to be ready to announce, at a precise moment in history, the appearance on earth of Jesus of Nazareth, the Savior of the world.

When the momentous moment came for Jesus to appear publicly to John, John recognized him by the Holy Spirit's revelation.

His voice rose in great awe and passion to the multitude who had been attracted by his ministry in and around the Jordan River. He declared of Jesus, "Behold the Lamb of God, which taketh away the sin of the world" (Jn. 1:29).

John saw Jesus first in his spirit (invisible), later with his eyes.

Describing this scene, the Bible says John was a voice crying in the wilderness (see Mt. 3:3)—not only the earthly wilderness, but the wilderness of men's souls.

> The revelation of the Holy Spirit
> came to me in these words, "John
> was not an *echo*, but a *voice*!"

That revelation was like an arrow to my heart. Abruptly, I turned from looking at other preachers as my models and depending on their sermon outlines. I threw everything out of my study chambers; picked up my Bible and my concordance; Bible dictionary; books by anointed writers on the Bible; special books on the Hebrew and Greek languages from which our King James translation and other translations were taken; and made a commitment that I would

- study myself full,

- pray myself anointed,

- hear from God directly in my spirit,

- and preach fresh, new sermons from my study of the Word and from my own experiences.

41

The third way I studied the Bible was to concentrate on special verses and passages about people's lives, their life experiences, and pronouncements of God's principles. From these I build my sermons and teachings. I include how I may respond or react in a given situation. Doing this helps me bring the Bible down to people as one person, or one family, making it a direct application to them as though God is speaking to them individually. To me, preaching is not as much *about* something as it *is* something itself. I call this textual preaching.

I believe it is an advantage to select a text and subject based on the two first ways I've described of studying the Bible. Study it as a whole, getting the core teachings, the key verses, the bottom line, and a worldview. Study events as they fit into the whole of the Bible and God's answer to all the problems, hopes, and dreams of each one of us.

Studying the Bible in these ways formed my foundation and knowledge so that I can almost instantly know where I am at the moment in the Bible. In the text I choose, I can take my concordance and run down correlating Scriptures to balance it. I believe these *methods* of study are major reasons my ministry is *balanced* and has lasted for over a half century.

To become the original God intended me to be, I not only had to change my methods for studying the Bible, but I also had to receive *revelation knowledge* on how to incorporate the healing ministry into my preaching and teaching. For this, I studied how Jesus did it. Little did I know that this would help transform the world. I was about to see the invisible!

Teaching, Preaching, Healing—Transforming the World

God's words to me were, "Son, don't be like other men, don't be like other preachers, don't be like your denomination. You be like Jesus and heal and deliver the people as He did."

They really woke me up, causing me to see how much I had failed.

From the depths of my soul, I cried, "Lord, I don't know how to be like Jesus." He replied, "Read the four Gospels and the Book of Acts through three times consecutively in thirty days while on your knees, and I will show you how to be like Jesus."

No mentor in the ministry had talked to me like that. "Follow the line of your denomination, stick to the doctrine, learn to follow your church leaders—don't have an independent ministry" was what I heard constantly.

As I undertook to obey God's word of knowledge to me and got into the Gospels and the Acts with all my being, I had an awakening. I found that Jesus did not try to be like the religious hierarchy of His day. Far from it. He said He did nothing His Father had not told Him to do and said nothing He had not heard His Father say. (See John 5:19; 8:28.) He had a straight line to His Father, which I did not. I was not attuned that way.

I read books of theology, and books of sermons by other preachers, and I learned to preach many of those sermons. I was not looking directly to Jesus as my example in ministry. I was somebody else, not the original God intended me to be, and I was miserable. My results were pitiful when compared with the ministry of Jesus and His disciples.

As soon as I was down on my knees reading Matthew, Mark, Luke, John, and the Acts, focused on Jesus, I saw that I had fallen short. My way of ministry was not His way. That was why I was such a poor example of one of His "called" preachers and was having such poor results, not the kind of results that He had in delivering the lost and suffering.

As I finished my third reading of the four Gospels, an amazing thing happened. The best way I can describe it is that

Jesus, as He really is, stood up on the pages of these all-important books (the only original information we have about Jesus' life and ministry on earth). By a way I don't understand, I saw *Him*!

I felt He had shown Himself to me. There He was—walking the dusty roads, visiting the towns in the land that Abraham had known, and going into Jerusalem, the Holy City, itself.

Before, I had seen Him more in parts, not as the cohesive whole man that He was. Now I had a clear picture of Jesus preaching, teaching, and healing, and doing them not separately but interchangeably. Then I knew that I knew to obey God's word "to be like Jesus," I had to change almost everything about my ministry, for I was not preaching, teaching, and healing interchangeably as He had done.

My preaching was far from the threefold method Jesus used as described in Matthew 4:23-25:

> *And Jesus went about all Galilee,* teaching *in their synagogues, and* preaching *the gospel of the kingdom, and* healing *all manner of sickness and all manner of disease among the people. And His fame went throughout all Syria: and they brought unto Him all sick people that were taken with divers diseases and torments, and those which were possessed with devils, and those which were lunatic, and those that had the palsy; and He healed them. And there followed Him great multitudes of people from Galilee, and from Decapolis, and from Jerusalem, and from Judaea, and from beyond Jordan.*

Here I saw that Jesus offered the "good news" of the gospel by preaching, teaching, and healing interchangeably.

44

He didn't just preach, or just teach, or just heal. He did them in harmony and as a whole approach of the gospel.

This pattern set Him apart as totally different from those who approached the needs of the people with a less than whole-person approach, leaving the people in their separation from God and the hurts and ills of their lives.

When Jesus appeared, they saw and felt in Him One who was in the struggle with them, One who sat where they sat, One who felt what they felt. By His preaching, teaching, and healing approach, He caused them to see God in an entirely new light.

- God is a good God,

- God is a near God and feels the infirmities of your spirit, body, and circumstances,

- God has power to change you and make you whole— new creatures, where old things pass away and all things become new. (See Second Corinthians 5:17.)

The net effect of Jesus' threefold gospel approach opened people's hearts, softened their attitude toward God, and gave them a vision that their lives could be changed—not just an opportunity to join a denomination and be like other religious people without the miraculous power of God in their lives.

After Jesus' resurrection and the outpouring of the gift of the Holy Spirit on the Day of Pentecost, the Book of Acts tells us of how the apostles, and even deacons, taught, preached, and healed interchangeably. They literally followed in Jesus' footsteps. The world could not resist them, and this Christian faith spread throughout the world.

Well, when I came along, this meshing of teaching, preaching, and healing no longer existed in the Body of Christ.

I do not know all the reasons. I was not present in all the generations from Jesus' to mine. All the Church history I had read centered around the perpetuation of the gospel in various ways by many different groups who believed in the Lord Jesus Christ, but largely without the combination of the three-part ministry example of Jesus and His early followers.

Seldom have I heard preaching that follows Jesus' method and practice. Consequently, few preachers see results like those enjoyed by Jesus or the anointed preachers we read about in the Book of Acts.

An overwhelming desire filled me to change, no matter the cost to my position or my present way of ministering. Even if it meant giving up the ministry and getting a job in the secular world, I was ready to stop being an echo, rather than a voice of the Lord. I now saw and felt about people in an entirely different way.

I desperately wanted to be part of their life struggles, to feel

- their sins,

- their sicknesses and diseases,

- their lack of the necessities of life,

- their having no contact with a preacher who would sit where they sit, feel what they feel, and who had the power of God in his life and ministry to offer them what Jesus did: *the more abundant life.* (See John 10:10.)

I began a new study of the ministry methods of Jesus and His first followers. As a result, I started teaching on healing a little more. I prayed for a few sick folk but I saw no definite miracle.

An exception came in the eleventh year of my ministry when I was pastoring in Toccoa, Georgia. A deacon of my church, Clyde Lawson, owned an automobile repair shop. One day when I was sharing with Bill Lee, another deacon, in the church office, I received a frantic phone call from Mrs. Lawson. "Come quick," she cried over the phone. "Clyde has been badly hurt."

We rushed to his shop. Mrs. Lawson met us, telling us she had called their doctor and he was coming as soon as he could. She led us into the shop where Clyde was lying on the floor, twisting and writhing. Holding his right foot in his hands, he was screaming in terrible pain.

As he was carrying a heavy motor across the floor, it had slipped from his hands and fallen on his foot, cutting through the shoe and crushing his foot.

Without conscious thought and before I realized what I was doing, I reached down and touched his shoe where the blood was coming out. "Heal, O Lord," I said almost under my breath, and straightened back up.

Suddenly Clyde Lawson stopped writhing on the floor, released his foot from his hands, stood up, stomped his foot, and said, "Oral Roberts, what did you do to me?"

By this time I was frightened out of my wits. "Nothing. I didn't do anything."

"Yes, you did! The pain is gone! I'm healed!"

He pulled off his shoe, and his foot was perfectly normal, with just a little blood left on it.

I quickly turned to leave. When we got in the car, Bill Lee said, "Pastor, God healed him when you stooped down and prayed. Can you do this all the time?"

"Good Lord, no," I answered.

"Well, if you could, you could bring God's healing power to His people."

The news of that healing spread as Clyde testified in the church and to others. As for me, I was perplexed. What I had done was not on purpose but because of a compassion I had suddenly felt sweep through me. It was as though an unseen power had pulled me down to touch his foot and say my little prayer.

After this happened, new questions came to my mind. *Why, Lord, why? Where is Your healing power for our day? When is it going to return as in the days of the early Christian Church?*

As I continued my pastoral and evangelistic ministry, the possibility of healing returning to the Body of Christ grew in my mind and spirit, but unfortunately not in my practice. I was growing in my teaching and preaching, but healings were still absent from my efforts. *Now that I had seen the invisible, how in the world was I going to do the impossible?*

Although Evelyn knew I was called to preach, I had not shared with her my calling into the *healing* ministry. Still, she knew something was going on between God and me.

One night she asked me to sit down on the side of the bed and tell her what was going on. I said, "Evelyn, 12 years ago when I was 17 the Lord had just saved me and healed me of terminal tuberculosis and of a stuttering tongue. God said to me, 'You are to take My healing power to your generation,' and I don't know how to do it."

She said, "Oh yes you do, Oral."

A light went on in my spirit. I said, "Okay, I do. Don't cook for me anymore until I tell you. I've got to have this out with God."

After having fasted and prayed, I went to my little church office, closed the door, lay face down on the floor, and told God I would not get up until He spoke to me on *how* I was to obey His bidding.

After hours, I do not know how many, God spoke, "Stand upon your feet." So I stood up and waited. Then He said, "Go get in your car, drive one block east and turn right, and I will tell you what to do."

As I turned the corner, He said,

"From this hour you will have My power to bring healing to the sick, and to cast out demons. You will know their number and name and have My power to cast them out."

When I reached home, I rushed in and told Evelyn, "Cook me a meal! I've just heard from the Lord."

My Time Has Come!

When I started ministering to the sick, carrying out the third part of Jesus' threefold method of ministry, a new anointing and power instantly came into my teaching and preaching.

It was as though I went to bed *without* this new anointing and power and woke up *with* it. It's probably not that simple, but I know it did not come *gradually*. When I stood up to preach in my pastorate, none of my sermon outlines fit. A whole new understanding of my long study of the Bible and of the inner hunger of my soul came forth as I opened my mouth to preach.

49

A new sermon came to me: "If You Need Healing, Do These Things." There I was—a novice attempting to tell the people their need of healing could be met and here's how. Looking back at that moment, I wonder how I could have been so daring—or so foolish.

I seemed to be outside myself listening to the ideas and words flowing out of my mouth.

The Holy Spirit was energizing my spirit, mind, and body as I had never known. I felt like I was on fire and couldn't stand still. The power of God was flowing into and out of me. The people were leaning forward in the pews, hanging on to every word from their pastor. They suddenly knew I was a different man, an anointed man, a God-possessed man.

When I closed the sermon, scores rushed forward to be prayed for. Some fell under the power of God. Some were crying so hard they were beside themselves. Others had a holy laugh coming out of them. There was no pandemonium, just serious calling out to God for His miracle touch.

I finally had caught fire with the spirit of the healing Jesus, and I began to teach/preach/heal simultaneously.

I became a person God was going to use to help bring back the original way of giving the gospel, just as Jesus and His first followers had.

In Jesus' day, His miracles and healings among the people seemed to overshadow His preaching and teaching. But He meshed His *preaching*, *teaching*, and *healing* into a togetherness, a harmonious whole. Eventually the attraction of the miracles and healings drew multitudes to hear Him who otherwise would not have come to listen to Him. It seemed to me their hearts had to be touched before their minds could be reached.

In a far smaller way, as I became a voice, an original that God Himself was making, the miracles and healings attracted my generation to hear the preaching and teaching. The healings paved the way, and made possible all the accomplishments—so amazing to me still—that have come forth from my ministry. Because I saw the invisible, the impossible became possible, enabling me not to be an echo or a fly-by-nighter, but one who has endured and whose work is destined to last.

My counsel to anyone is in all your reading, studying, and preparation of mind and spirit to fulfill God's call on your life, look in the mirror and observe who you see. Determine who you really are, meditate on who you wish to become. Although you should respect other leaders and can learn many things from them, come to a definite point where you realize:

- you are to be an *original*,

- you are somebody,

- you are chosen by the Lord God of Heaven and earth, of time and eternity, so strive with all of your being to become more and more like Jesus.

Continually attempt to do your ministry as He did by preaching, teaching, and healing interchangeably, never leaving one out, but seeing man as he is in his fallen and lost condition: in need of being made whole by the power of God.

We are taught to be subject to those who have authority over us. (See Hebrews 13:7.) But the supreme authority is your personal Savior and Lord, Jesus Christ of Nazareth, who died on the cross in your place, rose from the dead for your salvation, and sent the Holy Spirit to reveal His call upon your life.

You're not going to be perfect.

Setbacks,

shortcomings,

dumb mistakes,

and falling short will seek to plague you and dog your steps—just like they did me.

51

When the Holy Spirit convicts you of missing the mark, just turn to First John 1:9: "If we confess our sins, He is faithful and just to forgive us our sins, and to cleanse us from all unrighteousness."

I have my moments when everything I do seems to be flawless, without mistakes, wholly consecrated. I have my moments when I fall so far short that I hug First John 1:9 to my breast and weep and confess my weaknesses and failures to Him. I've found that He is faithful to forgive me and to cleanse me from *all* unrighteousness.

Paul's great word to us all is a great help to me.

Brethren, I count not myself to have apprehended: but this one thing I do, forgetting those things which are behind, and reaching forth unto those things which are before, I press toward the mark for the prize of the high calling of God in Christ Jesus (Philippians 3:13-14).

One thing for sure, Oral Roberts has not arrived. But with all my heart I am on the way, trying with all of my spirit, mind, body, and emotions to be more like Jesus and to do ministry the way He did it.

Can we do any more?

IMPORTANT POINTS

1. Be an original—a voice, not an echo.

2. Minister as Jesus did, in wholeness. Teach, preach, and heal interchangeably.

3. Study the Bible in full spectrum—from beginning to end, event by event. See these events meshing, leading you more and more toward Jesus in His method of teaching, preaching, and healing interchangeably.

4. Be alert to see the invisible so you can know that you know you can do the impossible.

6

How I Learned Not to Quit

L ooking back at the first year of my saving and healing ministry, I am still embarrassed by how close I came to walking out of one of my crusades within months after I started.

After hearing of astonishing results of my first effort to preach, teach, and heal interchangeably, a group of ministers drove down from Chanute, Kansas, to Tulsa to be in one of my services. They prevailed upon me to bring my ministry to the 4,000-seat auditorium in their city where they would be my sponsors.

In the middle of that three-week crusade, the building was filled night after night, and both the numbers of conversions and healings were very encouraging. This was only seven months after I had begun the healing ministry.

No one had guaranteed to cover the cost of the auditorium, the hotel rooms, and needs for my small team, not to mention anything to support my family. Carried away by the faith that filled my heart, I thought I could believe God for anything.

Imagine my shock when the finance committee of the sponsoring pastors announced to me that the offerings from the evening services were running below the rental costs of the auditorium alone. I said, "Let me receive the offering tonight." I was the leader, I was being accepted, and I had no doubt that when I mentioned the need, the people would contribute generously. All bills would be paid before we fell further behind.

Admittedly, I had never faced the budget of a crusade of this magnitude. But I was sailing right along, completely focused on carrying out what I was convinced Jesus wanted me to do.

Well, when I presented the needs of the meeting and later was given a slip of paper telling how much four thousand people had given, *my faith fell flat and my heart sank.* Although we had been paying the rental fees weekly, I realized the response of that evening would make it impossible to pay the bill. I was knocked for a loop.

All my life I had fought a quick temper—words came out of my mouth before I could call them back. I thought that my obedience and faith had propelled me into an entirely new level, breaking me out of the old mold, and that nothing could disturb my peace of mind.

Right there behind the platform, with that little slip of paper in my hand, my insides turned inside out. Anger flew all over me. Before I could stop them, words flew out of my mouth. "I quit. I'm not going to get up there and preach tonight. I'm going back to Tulsa." I turned to leave the building.

My brother Vaden said, "Oral, where are you going?"

"Back to Tulsa," I replied.

"You're not leaving the meeting?"

"I am."

"Stay right here; I'll be right back."

When he returned, he had Evelyn with him. She said, "Oral, what's the matter?"

I handed her the slip of paper. Burning inside, I said, "Evelyn, if I can't trust God for finances, I can't trust Him for anything else. I'm getting out of here."

"Oral, you can't do that," she said.

"Watch me," I replied.

Evelyn was a quiet woman, devoted to the Lord, and to me and our children, and had no doubt whatsoever that I was called of the Lord for the whole-person ministry. She also knew how nearly fanatical I was about financial integrity and that I couldn't abide unpaid bills.

She said, "Vaden, hold him right here. I'll be back soon." She had never faced a crowd like this before. The next voice I heard was hers, asking to borrow a man's hat. Then I heard her say over the microphone, "Friends, I'm embarrassed to be standing here with this hat in my hand, but I know my husband. The ministers' committee, then he, have asked for your financial support sufficiently to pay all bills whether he receives anything for his ministry or not."

I heard her voice break as she said, "I know my husband. He feels his faith has failed, and if he doesn't have enough faith to believe for the finances, he's closing the meeting tonight and returning home." She was crying.

"Please understand that he is an honest man. He's giving you his very best, and it is the Lord who has sent him here to help bring His saving and healing power to you. You've seen with your own eyes what God can do. But now you have a decision to make."

By this time I had dropped my head and was pushing Vaden away. "Wait! Wait!" he said.

I had walked away and left things to my wife. I knew she would rather do anything in the world than ask that crowd to help. The last words I heard Evelyn say really shamed me.

"I'm going to ask that someone take this hat among you. I believe you haven't realized what it takes for a meeting of this size to meet all its bills and not leave anything unpaid. My husband is that kind of man. Please," and here she broke down.

I started up to get her and help her off the stage when a large red-haired woman with a strong voice stood up. Her words rolled across the entire building. "I'm ashamed of everyone in this audience, especially of myself. I'm the mother of several children. We have lots of needs and the Lord has met many of these needs through His servant Oral Roberts. Now you listen to me; I want every one of you to do what I'm going to do." Then she opened her purse, pulled out a worn dollar bill, put it in the hat, and sat down. In a few moments people were standing and saying, "Mrs. Roberts, bring that hat over here."

I was feeling lower and lower but stood transfixed as others popped up, some weeping, and said, "Here, I'll help."

Evelyn saw me and put her arm around me. Crying, she said, "Oral, you've got the faith. Don't give up on it now."

My inner man was still not standing up. "Have them count the offering," I said. "I'll wait."

Several men jumped up and started counting the money, which was now overflowing the big ranch-type hat. Soon one of them ran down the aisle and called out, "How much was needed?" I pointed to the sponsoring pastors. One of them told the man. A big smile came on his face. Pointing to the microphone, he asked Evelyn, "Can I say a word over that thing?"

With one hand raised for the crowd to listen and the other on the mike stand, he announced there was more than enough to pay the auditorium rental and all other bills to that time.

To my surprise, a shout went up and the crowd began hollering to me, "Preach! Preach!"

I said to myself, "Oral Roberts, get back to that microphone and preach the gospel as you've never done before!" And I did!

I had been tempted for a while that night to throw in the towel and go back on my calling. But I had seen that the Lord wasn't going to let the devil defeat us, not even financially.

I now knew faith would find a way.

That was in November 1947. In May 1969, when Oral Roberts University was graduating its first freshman class, among them was a young man who was graduating summa cum laude with a 4.0 average.

Handing him his diploma for a B.A. degree, I realized who he was. He was the son of a black pastor, one of the sponsoring pastors of the Chanute, Kansas, crusade and had been a baby in his mother's arms at that time.

With his proud parents sitting nearby, I told the audience of that night in Chanute when I had come so close to throwing it all away. From that hour my faith had grown stronger and stronger. Because I had not quit, young men and women coming out of ORU through the years could have faith, integrity, and commitment to excellence and obedience to God.

At the time of the Kansas crusade, I was 29 years old. I was young, quick-tempered, and sometimes rash, but the Lord knew just what it took to step into the breach and save the ministry that was striving to be like His Son's, Jesus Christ of Nazareth.

I was not proud of myself that night in Chanute. Although I already loved Evelyn with a passion, that was the first time I publicly called her "my darling wife, Evelyn." And I've done that ever since.

Evelyn later wrote a book, titled, *His Darling Wife, Evelyn*, which became a best-seller.

What I'm trying to say is that things aren't always going to be even. There are rough spots ahead. They will often catch you by surprise. You may or may not know how to handle them at the moment. You may feel like quitting as I did.

The thing I learned was that God will make a way where there seems to be no way.

You can count on Him!

IMPORTANT POINTS

1. Don't quit no matter how you *feel*.

2. Don't act rashly. Think of the long-term results of your actions.

3. Remember that you can count on God to come through.

4. Faith will find a way!

5. God will have others to help you.

7

How I Discovered God Is a Healing God

The revelation came into my spirit that the God who saves is also the God who heals.

As a young preacher reading and studying the Bible, I learned that God's principle of healing was inextricably interwoven with His principle of forgiving people of their sins. It amazes me that I didn't connect the two as interchangeable—saving and healing.

I came to realize that the God I serve is a *healing* God and that in my ministry I should have compassion for the sick. This compassion would drive me to bring forth their faith to be healed through my preaching (see Rom. 10:17), and to be an anointed *point of contact* between them and our healing Lord.

I began my journey of bringing God's healing power to hurting people with miraculous results, which almost immediately brought me from obscurity to the attention of the national news media, and to the attention of a large segment of the Christian Church nationally and worldwide.

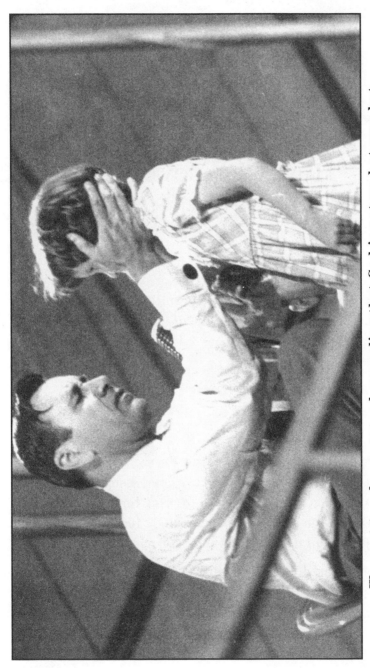

We must tread new ground, revealing that God is not mad at man but that as a good God He came with life-saving power—not just for their souls, but also for their body, mind, finances, and family.

With this attention also came controversy such as I had never known. At first I allowed it to scare me almost out of my wits—and my calling. Like a lone ranger I was treading new ground, revealing that God is not mad at man. As a good God, He came with life-saving power—not just for the soul, but for the body, mind, finances, and family, also.

Now I had a desperate longing to come face-to-face with sick and suffering people. I prayed for their healing, laying hands on them regardless of the disease, contagious or not. God protected me for 21 uninterrupted years of a world healing ministry in which I personally laid hands on more than a million and a half individuals who had "all manner of sickness...and disease" (Mt. 4:23b). I also engaged the demon spirits in tens of thousands, calling to them, "Come out, you foul, tormenting spirits of satan, and let this person go free!"

By the seventh year I brought a film crew inside the big 10,000-seat tent cathedral and in auditoriums and stadiums to film *live* the actual healing line. Some two hundred of the most powerful television stations sold us broadcast time to bring the healing Jesus directly into millions of homes. There people saw healing for the first time since the days when Jesus and His disciples *publicly* healed the sick, cast out demon spirits, and brought "the more abundant life" to the people.

In the late 1940s, only a handful of us preached healing like this. Today there are thousands of ministers who teach, preach, and heal interchangeably—including those who graduate from ORU, a major university, fully accredited academically and anointed in every aspect with the saving and healing power of the living Christ.

Today I have the privilege of seeing thousands of Oral Roberts University graduates being "raised up to hear God's

Word, to go where His light is seen dim, His power is not known, and where their work will exceed mine, in which God is well pleased." With my son, Richard, the second president, doing a better job operating ORU than I did, my life is complete as I'm finishing my course.

How Do You Receive Your Healing?

I would be remiss if I did not share with you the steps God revealed to me for receiving your healing.

First, see God's anointed ministers as instruments of bringing His teaching, preaching, and healing to you. Look beyond them to Him who is invisible until you see the invisible. Then see in your spirit that all things are possible as you believe—including the miracle of healing in your body.

Second, seek to hear the men and women of God who follow Jesus' example of teaching, preaching, and healing interchangeably. Understand that although you have faith (see Rom. 12:3), that faith must come forth and go to God as Paul said. "Faith cometh by hearing, and hearing by the word of God" (Rom. 10:17).

Third, get a *point of contact*, something you do to release your faith when you receive healing prayer. Everything in life has a point where you contact it. The light switch is the point of contact to the power plant so that when you touch the switch the lights come on. Turning the key in your car is the point of contact that turns the motor on and the car starts, ready for you to drive.

Likewise, God's healing power has points of contact which you *do*. When you *do* one of them, you release your faith directly to God, making contact with the power that spins the universe. You touch the living Jesus, in whom is all miracle healing.

> Your healing starts at that instant
> your faith goes up to God.

Fourth, what you did to get your healing is what you continue to do to *keep* your healing. Throughout the Bible God tells us, "The just shall live by faith" (Gal. 3:11; Rom. 1:17; Hab. 2:4; Heb. 10:38). I also tell people, "We live by faith or die by doubt."

Your faith begins to move, to act, when the power of God supernaturally empties you of doubt and fills you with a knowing. You come into a state of knowing that you know that you know. In that instant **you cannot doubt!**

These are the exact words God gave me when I first asked Him to explain faith to me. This experience with faith has produced a *knowing* inside me, from time to time, ever since. It seems in that period of knowing I cannot doubt. It can happen to you, too, if you seek God for it. When you seek Him,

- expect Him to hear you,

- expect Him to give you this *knowing* of faith inside you,

- and keep expecting to receive so when He sends your miracle you will *recognize* it, take it inside yourself, and not let it pass you by.

Fifth, never, never doubt your own faith. You may wonder if you have faith. You do, for Paul said, "God hath [given] to every man the measure of faith" (Rom. 12:3).

Faith is not something you have to get. It's something you already have. Act on it by releasing it to God. That's when your healing starts.

IMPORTANT POINTS

1. Do what God calls you to do even when it is not popular.

2. Live by faith or die by doubt.

3. Get a point of contact to release your faith.

4. Ask the Holy Spirit to supernaturally empty you of doubt and fill you with a knowing that you will be healed, so that in that moment you cannot doubt. Whether you're under medical care or receiving healing prayer, have that *knowing* in your heart. Remember, a double-minded man is unstable in all his ways (see Jas. 1:8).

*   As you "hear" anointed preaching of the Word, it causes your faith to "come up" inside you, so you can release it to God.

*   Remember Jesus' teaching, preaching, and healing are going on all the time simultaneously. His healing power is coming toward you, or past you, so expect a miracle. Recognize it, reach out, and receive it! Don't let it pass you by! Knowing that God *wants* to heal you is all-important to you.

8

How I Learned to Preach With the Anointing Every Time

I regret that as a young preacher, all too often I preached without the anointing. In fact, I didn't know what the anointing was, let alone be able to preach with this miraculous indwelling of the very presence of God, as if He were there in person making my words and efforts come alive.

I had read about the anointing in the Bible. From the first week of my conversion and healing, I had been given an insatiable thirst to know God in me. I reasoned that if He had changed my one little insignificant life, He had a thousand more things He could do in and through me, *if I only knew* how!

The power of anointing stood out to me as I read how men spoke and acted for God. I was impressed that every time they spoke or acted in His name, mighty things happened. It was through seeing the invisible that they could accomplish the impossible.

This was clear all through the Old Testament account and came to a climax when Jesus began His earthly ministry. His followers carried it on in the founding of the Christian Church.

Luke, the beloved physician, told how Jesus started His ministry:

The Spirit of the Lord is upon Me, because He hath anointed Me to preach the gospel to the poor; He hath sent Me to heal the brokenhearted, to preach deliverance to the captives, and recovering of sight to the blind, to set at liberty them that are bruised (Luke 4:18).

And in Acts he described how Jesus continued His ministry:

How God anointed Jesus of Nazareth with the Holy Ghost and with power: who went about doing good, and healing all that were oppressed of the devil; for God was with Him (Acts 10:38).

Jesus never attempted to preach—or do anything in His calling—without the Spirit of the Lord being upon Him and the power of anointing flowing through His words and actions. When I first saw this, I knew I had been on the wrong track as a young preacher.

The impact of the anointed preaching of the gospel in those who preached in Bible days came because they had been with Jesus.

I thought, *I've been with Jesus too*. He came to my bed of illness and so powerfully saved my soul and healed me. I was a new creation. The old Oral Roberts was gone, the new man in Christ had emerged in my life. It was unmistakable. Never would I doubt that I had passed from death unto life, from darkness to light.

My biggest mistake was overlooking the power of anointing *for me*. I nearly missed out on it altogether. I saw it in Jesus, in His followers, then in my father who talked about the

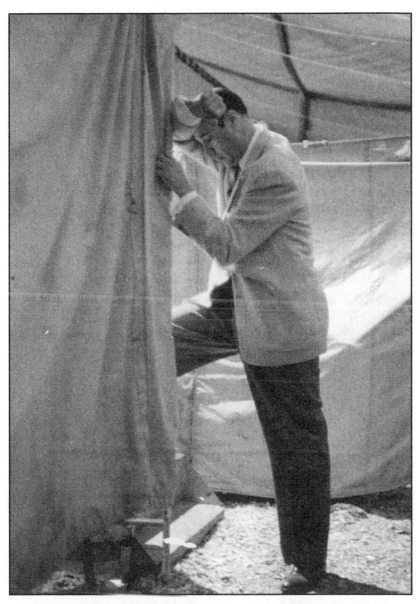

We should never overlook the power of the anointing God has for us. Before I attempt to do anything for God, I cry out in prayer for His anointing.

anointing making all the difference in his preaching the gospel.

Yet there *were* times I was acutely aware during my sermons that the Spirit of the Lord was all over me. A divine power had hold of my being. Words flowed out of me in what we now call revelation knowledge.

It was the power of anointing on me, and it began to change the impact of my preaching. I could tell when I was anointed and when I wasn't. The difference in results was easy to see. Since my burning desire was to obey God and bring Him to the needs of the people, I began to realize I'd better find a way to preach with the anointing every time. But how?

I thought, *I can't make the anointing come upon me. Or could I? What had I done to cause the anointing to come when it did, and what had I failed to do when it hadn't?*

I saw that having the anointing on my words and actions made such a difference (really it made all the difference), that I stopped my ministry studies and appointments and got off to myself, saying, "I'm going to have this out with God."

During a period of several days, I pounded myself with questions:

- Why does the anointing come on me at times, and not every time?

- How was the anointing opening me up?

- How was it opening the Bible up more than my usual studies did?

- How was I missing out on this?

I certainly was no less close to God. I loved Him with everything in me.

My entire focus was to fulfill His call on my life.

What else could I do?

One day I asked my preacher-father these questions. He was not nearly as educated as I was. He knew far less of the history and geography of the Bible than I did. He was not able to put the events of the Bible together in every book in the Bible as I had learned to do, yet when he preached, the Spirit of the Lord was all over him. When the power of anointing came on him, he had a habit of reaching up and taking hold of his left earlobe. From that moment you felt something surge through you. You knew God was there.

When Papa made his invitation to people to come forward and make their decision for Christ, some literally *ran* forward. It was a moving sight for a young preacher.

When I asked him about the anointing, Papa said, "Son, the Bible is not just ink and paper. Without the Holy Spirit giving you *insight* from above...without the Spirit of God inspiring you...without God's anointing taking charge of you, you'll never really preach the Word of God!"

"But, Papa, how can I cause this to happen in me every time as you do?"

"How much do you want it, Oral?"

"With all my heart."

"Then vow to God that you won't get in the pulpit until you first feel the anointing of God's Spirit coming upon you and permeating your being."

"Can I really do this?"

"I do it."

"Anytime?"

"Son, I would no more think of trying to preach the unsearchable riches of the gospel without the power of God coming upon me than I would consider trying to live without eating."

Wow! This statement hit me like a ton of bricks.

Papa said, "As much as you're studying your Bible, don't you see how the anointing is the principal thing in all Jesus did, in all His apostles did, and in all those you hear today whose ministry is changing lives for the Lord?"

Slowly, I nodded, yes. I realized he knew the *key issue*, the main thing for a young preacher, really for all preachers. I'm so grateful to have had a father like my dad.

I went back to my Bible, with my concordance, and sought out the terms, "the Spirit of the Lord, the anointing, the power of the Lord," and terms like these. By the time I finished, the power of anointing was so all-important, it got hold of my whole being. Right then and there I vowed to God I would never again attempt to preach His gospel without first feeling His anointing coming into my body. I would feel the anointing, at least to some extent, or I wouldn't get up to preach.

What did I do next? Several things I'll quickly describe, but none as important as the vow I made to be anointed every time I preached. *Later I enlarged my vow to cover every important decision I was trying to make:*

I would have the anointing or
I would not make the decision!

First, I finally understood that the anointing is the main thing. I learned, as my dear anointed friend and preacher, Joyce Meyer, says, the main thing is the main thing, and there's no substitute. The anointing on each of us is the power of God working in us to deliver the people.

Secondly, I got literal with my vow. When the temptation came and I did not begin to feel the anointing, I refused to minister. I said, "God, if You can't touch me as I prepare to preach and let me experience the Spirit of the Lord going through me, causing me to feel at least some of Your anointing, I'm not going to preach this sermon."

Believe me, satan tempted me on this over and over—sometimes by forgetfulness, sometimes by being in a hurry, sometimes by being called on when I was not expecting it.

I began to learn how wholly concerned God is that I did not attempt to preach on just what *I knew*, or just depending on myself. That was a big temptation!

I began to learn just how much more powerful, how much nearer He was to me, and that I did not have to compromise.

I know of no greater compromise satan has hit us with than being willing to go ahead and preach without the anointing.

Some church leaders got angry at me when I refused their requests. Some thought I had not prepared myself in the Word of God. (They were wrong.) Some thought I was scared to preach without the anointing. (They were right.)

The big test came in Philadelphia, Pennsylvania, in July 1950, at the old Metropolitan Auditorium. The crusade was going great, with powerful results. My precious brother, Reverend R. W. Schambach, at age 19, got his first experience with my ministry at that crusade. Several other ministers, who later became prominent in ministering God's power, have told me

Jesus didn't preach or minister without having the certainty of the anointing, and neither should you.

that they were exposed to and impacted by my ministry at that time.

In my hotel room that day, I could not get the mind of the Lord on what to preach; neither could I feel His Spirit flowing through me during my studies and prayer. By the time the driver knocked on my door that it was time to go, I was sitting up in a chair, my arms folded across my chest, my mind made up. His anointing hadn't begun in me, not once during that entire day. There I sat.

Thousands were expecting me to preach with the power of God,

to be anointed to lead souls to Christ,

to pray for the sick and get results.

And I felt nothing. My mind was a blank— except for one thing: *my vow.*

My associates knew of my vow not to preach without the anointing. So when I didn't show up the first hour of one of the crusade services with a packed audience waiting, they didn't get alarmed. But my driver did.

I went to the door and told him just to find a place to wait. He said, "If we don't go now, you'll be late."

"Just wait. I'll either come or let you know I'm not coming."

Sitting back down, putting my hands on my knees, I said, "Lord Jesus, You didn't preach without first having the certainty of the anointing. You know my vow. It's up to You now."

And there I sat feeling like the loneliest man in the world. Satan whispered, "If you don't show up at the auditorium, what will the people think?" I refused to answer.

Time passed, and I sat there, my vow intact, knowing what worth I would be to those hurting people without the power of anointing.

Suddenly I heard God's voice. As usual, it was the clearest of all voices I ever heard. "Son, do you know just what My anointing is?" I didn't move an eyelash.

He said, "The anointing is when you're separated from yourself and filled with My glory, so that when you speak it's like I am speaking; when you act, it's like I am acting."

I'd never heard it that clearly before, but at that moment I knew that this was exactly what the anointing is.

I remained sitting there. I felt nothing, but I knew I had heard the real thing. I knew it was true, absolutely true.

The Spirit of the Lord came all over me in an instant, down my right arm into my right hand. My mind was illuminated. The message I had been worrying with all day became as clear as the noonday sun. I jumped up, grabbed my Bible, and dashed out the door.

My driver was walking the hall, beside himself. "Come on," I said. "I'm anointed!"

Will I ever forget what happened when I entered that auditorium? People felt the presence of God all over the place. Involuntarily they stood. Many began to weep. I entered the pulpit, and His Holy Spirit took over. The results of that service live in my heart to this hour. If I needed convincing to pay the price, and to preach with the anointing every time, it was answered once and for all.

Consider with me, if you will, the state of what the world knows the Christian Church to be. See it through their eyes, their ears, their perception. Consider how they judge its condition by each of us in the ministry, young and old, and also by its lay members.

What do you think they think of us? When they come in contact with us, do they sense the anointing, the miraculous experience of being separated from ourselves, seeing the glory of Jesus so that when we speak or act it's like Jesus is doing it in person?

I can only speak for myself. My vow still holds to preach with the anointing every time. It's not always easy. My mind seeks to take over and control my thoughts, ignoring my vow. Carnality creeps in. When that happens, I'm just saying words. They're not getting into people's spirits (where they really are).

You may say, "Can I be anointed to do what God has called me to do?" *It's your decision*. You must believe you can do what Jesus did, have the same anointing He did. Maybe you haven't reached that place in your ministry I believe without a doubt that you can if you will to do it.

IMPORTANT POINTS

1. Don't overlook the power of anointing God has for you.

2. Don't make a decision without God's anointing.

3. The anointing is when you're separated from yourself and filled with God's glory, so that when you speak it's like God speaking; when you act, it's like God acting.

4. Know you can preach with the anointing every time.

5. Consider prayerfully the loss the people suffer if you preach even once without the anointing.

6. Think about it: would Jesus use the anointing but deny your earnest desire—your vow—to be anointed, also?

7. Remember, if Oral Roberts got the anointing, you can get it, too.

8. My advice: Don't go into the pulpit without it!

Part Two

Doing the Impossible

9

HOW SEEING THE INVISIBLE HELPED ME CHOOSE GOD'S DESTINY FOR MY LIFE OVER MY OWN DESIRES

E veryone faces a decisive choice in one way or another at different times in life. None of us are strangers to choices. Most of us ultimately realize that what choice we make determines which way our lives go and what happens to us. This is an inescapable fact of existence. Most of the time, it takes seeing the invisible to be able to choose the right way—God's destiny for your life. It certainly was that way for me.

My grandfather Amos Pleasant Roberts, who had brought the Oklahoma branch of the Roberts from Alabama following the Civil War and became a frontier judge in Indian Territory before it became the state of Oklahoma, had captivated and inspired my childhood. I was drawn to the political arena and dreamed of becoming a lawyer and governor of Oklahoma someday.

It soon became evident to some of the individuals running for public office in Pontotoc county that I had a natural bent toward politics.

I had accepted God's call to preach the gospel but that yearning to follow my childhood dream was still embedded in me.

It was a very real temptation.

Even after I had been in the ministry for two or three years, I had hired out to help certain men run for county and congressional positions, and for governor. They said I had a way about me that was effective in getting people to vote for them.

One summer I had been able to earn enough money from helping in political campaigns to buy my first car, a new Chevrolet coupe—with cash! I was also able to shed my ill-fitting clothes for better suits, shirts, and shoes for appearing in the pulpit. When I went to preach, I no longer looked like I needed everything myself. Instead, I hoped to inspire the people to believe that they could overcome their "dirt-poor" lives as I had.

In churches with a poverty mentality, I was criticized for owning a new car. Not only were they poor people, but for the most part they had no ambition or hope to rise from their conditions by their faith. They actually equated their condition with living a righteous life.

Because their children had to work in the fields to help feed their families, they were growing up with no education past grammar school. For the most part those children never received a high school or college advantage education.

The pastors were deeply resentful of anyone making good financially or having success in any area. Caught in a poverty syndrome, they couldn't seem to break out of it. They harbored a fear of emphasizing the goodness of God or His ownership of all the gold and silver in the earth and that God owned the earth and the fullness thereof (see Hag. 2:8; Ps.

24:1).Wrong teaching, low ambition, and fear seemed to "hide" the Word from them.

I felt that such a religious emphasis was unscriptural, thwarted legitimate ambition, held back progress, and condemned people to mediocrity and loss of hope. With all the odds against me, I finished high school (the only one of my family to do so), and eventually graduated from college and seminary.

So when I first started ministering, taking time off to earn enough money to get a head start in life appealed greatly to me.

When the candidates I had worked for, including the man running for governor, were elected, I was approached with two offers. One was to be groomed to run for the Oklahoma State Legislature at age 22. The other was to accept my choice of jobs in my area in Governor Leon C. Phillips' new office.

I came face-to-face with making the right or wrong decision at the most critical period of my young life in the ministry. I owed everything to God's saving and healing power, to His call on my life. Inside me was the unmistakable, unshakeable memory that in my father's face I had seen Him who is invisible. With all the preaching I had heard as a child and teenager, nothing moved my seared-over heart as that insight, which was beyond the natural. It was the turning point. Suddenly another voice was calling, this time much more interestingly. I felt that I could not see my childhood dreams being fulfilled in politics, which had been my life's ambition before.

Like everyone else, I had a will and the God-given power of choice. Jesus was on one side calling to me. Satan, whom I had been permitting to lead me in a totally different direction (see Jn. 10:10), was on the other. It's not that politics is wrong or a bad field to enter. What made it bad for me is that it wasn't God's choice for my life. That's what made all the difference.

I lacked maturity, but I knew the difference in the two ways of life I had had. I could do it my way—or I could understand, in the extremity of my situation, that Christ and His way was my answer.

I looked long and hard at the very real possibility of a political destiny in the face of the destiny to which Jesus now called me.

The political arena offered me relationships with highly placed leaders, more money than I had ever made, and a potential I had dreamed about. I admit it was very inviting, and the pull was very strong.

But I discovered in those hours and days of making my choice, "There's just something about that name," the name of my personal Savior and Lord, and the high purpose He had for my life and destiny.

I can empathize with people facing choices involving their way and God's way. In my own crucible I learned the incalculable value of the right choice.

Since the time I made my choice, I never again had a serious doubt that this ministry would survive and would do the impossible, all because I saw the invisible with my inner eyes and knew its powerful effect on my life. I saw it all through the Bible, and I found strength to face whatever other choice came my way. Without seeing the invisible and obeying God, I have no idea what my life would have turned out to be.

We serve a mighty God. He's not weak or distant, but an awesome God, closer to us than our breath, and constantly revealing Himself to us when we are open to Him. He shows us the invisible, which enables us to do the impossible.

In later experiences, I discovered that the impossible lay before me more than anyone thought. But, by faith, I knew I could and would do it.

IMPORTANT POINTS

1. Everyone faces a decisive choice in life—a choice of destiny. Be sure to choose God's destiny for you.

2. Choose the "more abundant" life in Jesus. Don't settle for mediocrity.

3. Remember, when God reveals His choice for your life, He never changes it. It is the only destiny that will enable you to do the impossible—to have peace of soul and of mind, without which life is not worth living.

4. Whether God chooses you for the ministry or some other calling, it is making the right choice, for His highest purpose, that makes the difference.

10

HOW I WAS LED TO GOD'S CHOICE OF A WIFE FOR ME

D uring my young days of traveling and preaching my new sermons, God began to deal with me on the kind of woman I was to marry. I began expecting that God had a young woman who saw things the way I did.

I had met Evelyn Lutman at our annual campmeeting where we played our guitars side by side in the youth services. I didn't know that two years later she would be the one I finally realized as God's choice of a wife for me.

She had written in her diary after that youth service, "I have met my future husband." Later she told me that, after she left the campmeeting and went back to finish college and become a teacher, she prayed, "Lord, I have no way of contacting Oral or even letting him know my feelings. If we marry, You'll have to let him know and bring us together." She was moving in the realm of faith which had become real to her, as it had become to me.

Two years later my father was assigned the pastorate in Evelyn's hometown, Westville, Oklahoma. Being single, I was still living at home. In the meantime, Evelyn had moved to the

Rio Grande Valley in Texas to live with her grandparents, the Wingates, to complete college and teach. She went to college during the summers and secured a country school job, teaching grades one through eight near Riviera, Texas.

I knew nothing of this as I traveled in and out of Westville to conduct revivals. Meanwhile, between my evangelistic travels, I had made a good friend of a man who attended the church and who was a successful trucker, owning his own rig. I went with him on some of his longer hauls. On one of these trips we got into a discussion on marriage. He told me he knew just the woman for me—Evelyn Lutman.

"Where is she?" I asked. I knew it was time for me to choose a helpmeet as the Bible had said.

"She's in Texas, teaching school. I'll get her address. You can drive down there in that shiny new Chevrolet you've just bought and check her out yourself," he told me.

"How do you know she'll want to see me? If she's the same girl I met at campmeeting two years ago, I really don't know her."

"She knows you, Oral Roberts."

"How could that be?"

"Boy," Frank said, putting his hand on his heart, "she knows you right in here."

"How could you know that?"

He just nodded his head, smiled, and kept on driving.

As I pondered this in my heart, I knew if Evelyn Lutman and I ever got together, it would have to be the Lord bringing us together. I wanted a wife like her, but I was trusting God for this most important move in my life...and in hers. *I was committed to obeying Him no matter the cost.*

I sent her a little booklet I had written, "Salvation by the Blood," and asked if I could call on her. She replied, "I'll be glad to see you."

Evelyn was six hundred miles away. My mother said, "If Oral is going that far to see a girl, then I'm going with him." And she did!

That was in September 1938. When I pulled up in front of her school, it was recess time. The little children said, "Miss Evelyn, your boyfriend is here!" She had gotten permission to leave early that Thursday, so we went to the Rio Grande Valley where her grandparents were fruit growers and exporters. They gave a warm welcome to me and also my mother.

Mama fell in love with Evelyn. She said, "Oral, this girl is a woman of substance. Also she is of our faith."

We spent the weekend getting acquainted. We went to church, and both of us went forward to pray.

We also went fishing on the Gulf of Mexico. *All we caught was each other.*

By the end of that long weekend, I knew in my deepest self that Evelyn was God's choice for me, and we got engaged. *We both had an inner knowing that God had put us together.* To me, that's the most important ingredient of any marriage.

When I returned to Oklahoma and to my ministry as an evangelist, we wrote each other almost daily. Actually, we fell in love through our letters. We felt love for each other that weekend but much more through our letters. In my opinion, communication—verbal, written, and in other ways—is vital.

> I have found no substitute for communication with one another.

Four months later, on Christmas Day at 3 p.m. in my father's church in Westville, Oklahoma, where Evelyn's parents lived, we were married. My close friend in the ministry, Oscar Moore, drove two hundred miles round-trip to perform the ceremony. I had borrowed $20 from a bank to get married. I paid $3 for the marriage license, $5 for flowers, and I gave Oscar $5.

From that time on, I gave Oscar Moore $100 every Christmas. Later I asked Oscar, "When do you think I will have made up for the $5 I gave you for your two hundred-mile round-trip to marry us?"

He smiled. "Oral, as soon as you think you've paid what Evelyn is worth."

I said, "Oscar, you wouldn't hold her priceless worth over my head, would you?"

Again he smiled. "Friend Oral, it's up to you." I kept on paying.

In the next chapter I want to give you seven keys that I trust are good, practical, and common sense to unlock the blessing and substance of a good marriage.

IMPORTANT POINTS

1. When you come face-to-face with the cost of commitment, pay it. It's worth it in the long run.

2. God wants commitment not only in our calling but in our personal lives as well. He sees us as a whole person.

3. In marriage, there is no substitute for communication with one another, not only in the beginning but also in all the years and decisions ahead.

11

SEVEN KEYS I LEARNED FOR A SUCCESSFUL MARRIAGE

Evelyn and I have been married for 63 years—successfully. I am reminded of the old saying,

Without God I cannot.

Without me He will not.

Anything undertaken for God is a divine/human reciprocity.

In this chapter I hope to present a formula that Evelyn and I can attest really works, and that pays enormous and lasting dividends. As I share these keys with you, it is with the understanding that we know we're not perfect. We have had to labor through many tight situations, be open with each other, and rely on our prayer life. Above all, we earnestly desire to honor God and uphold our own integrity—not only as ministers of the gospel, but as plain human beings.

Consider these seven keys that have opened the doors to a most precious and productive marriage for us.

KEY #1

We let God lead us to each other.

We never moved toward one another on our own but waited until we knew God's hand was bringing us together in ways we could not doubt were providential.

Each of us was convinced that God had the right spouse for us. Each of us was committed to looking to Him, rather than just following our own wisdom.

> I believe there is no substitute for marrying in God's will and in His time.

I realize that many readers may already be married; perhaps some of you were married before you began serving God.

Some marriages that seemed born in Heaven turn out disastrously, and some marriages that did not start off well have turned out great.

In our situation, Evelyn and I didn't stop with trusting God that we were marrying in His perfect will. This same commitment to go God's way was carried over by our wills into day-by-day life situations, and we continue that way to this day. Frankly, we both have worked at our marriage with no letup, and it's been worth it. I'm not talking about one of us working at it, but both of us. One can't carry the load alone, and sometimes marriage is a load. But with God's help, both partners can make the marriage succeed.

KEY #2

We married for life.

There was never any thought that if some serious trials came up we would part. We were married, *period*. Through these 63 years, not once have we considered separating or divorcing.

We're both baptized with the Holy Spirit. According to First Corinthians 6:19-20, the Holy Spirit has made our bodies His temple, we are bought with a price (Christ's shed blood), and we are God's property. That makes all the difference. We are literally not our own; we're His. We accept this, think this way, and feel He is our *covering*.

We're also basically engaged in "praying with the Spirit and with the understanding" as Paul taught and practiced (see 1 Cor. 14:1-3;13-15; Eph. 6:18).

The whole of each spouse's life has to be thought of in an inner sense.

Our union was first of all spiritual.

Although we are also physical and emotional, the spiritual is always paramount. After all, we are spiritual beings, with the physical body being the home of our spirit.

KEY #3

We found that being opposites in temperament is an integral part of our marriage success.

Evelyn is of German descent, very organized, thrifty, work motivated, and most of all, of a steady temperament. She is not easily upset or angered, and is able to bear a lot before she reaches the end of her endurance.

I'm just the opposite. As part Cherokee Indian, and the rest of Welsh descent, I'm quite combustible and quick-tempered. I say things before I think, and they often do harm for which I have to apologize and try to make right.

How often I've prayed that I could keep my big fat mouth closed a little longer!

But I'm blessed. Evelyn is the opposite. She helps to quiet me down, and she is wise enough to wait until I'm in a mood to listen to her.

Our differences work quite well together.

I am not methodical, except in the area of my ministry. She says she's never met a more creative and organized preacher than I am. In other areas of my life, I need help.

I handle the Lord's money very carefully (and some say wisely), but I'm not so skillful with our personal funds. For example, when we were in our thirties, she wanted me to put a certain amount, however small, in stocks, and then forget them until our old age. But no, I couldn't see it. As a result, we never built a substantial estate.

I could have done much better. I could have paid down on a duplex or fourplex to earn money for us. I could have driven our car a year or two longer. I could have resisted investing in a farm that kept us broke. Oh, I was a wise one, all right. But Evelyn with her German instincts knew better. She put up with my mistakes until I finally wised up. I realized that by my faith and diligence I could provide for our last years without having to depend on my family or Oral Roberts University.

We want to be a burden to no one, but to trust God to be our Source of total supply. We know by proven experience that if we remain faithful to sowing our tithe as a seed, expecting God's *miracle harvest returns*, all will be well. That's our faith and our goal. I am proud to say it is working.

KEY #4

We found that practicing a good sex life was connected far more closely to our spiritual development than we realized.

The first thing God said to man was, "Be fruitful, and multiply..." (Gen. 1:28). After the flood destroyed the human race and only Noah's family remained, God said to Noah and his sons, "Be fruitful, and multiply..." (Gen. 9:1).

But sex is for more than procreation to continue the human race. Sex is also for continual enjoyment of life and physical release.

In my study of the Bible, sex for procreation leaves us a half person only. Both male and female are created with unlimited ability—and desire—to bring themselves into being one person sexually.

Take that away, and man and woman in marriage, first being spiritual beings, rob themselves of the very necessary physical and emotional release God created them to have on a continuing basis.

Therefore, married couples should understand this and not feel inhibited in the sex act on a mutually worked-out basis that completes both.

Evelyn and I have thanked God many times for our understanding of this. It has contributed to the joyous success of our marriage, even into our later years.

Further, while sexual ability wanes in old age, as do all other functions of the body, we've found it important to our health and loving closeness to continue as often as possible.

The spiritual is always foremost, but the sexual is closely interwoven with the spiritual aspects of one's life.

A loving and consistent sex life that goes beyond childbearing is what I believe to be one of life's greatest fulfillments. Careful and consistent prayer and consideration must be given to it. I've known of too many otherwise promising marriages that shipwreck because of unfulfilled sex lives.

The explanation of the natural function of husband and wife is given by the apostle Paul in First Corinthians 7:1-5:

Now concerning the things whereof ye wrote unto me: It is good for a man not to touch a woman. Nevertheless, to avoid fornication, let every man have his own wife, and let every woman have her own husband. Let the husband render unto the wife due benevolence: and likewise also the wife unto the husband. The wife hath not power of her own body, but the husband: and likewise also the husband hath not power of his own body, but the wife. Defraud ye not one the other, except it be with consent for a time, that ye may give yourselves to fasting and prayer; and come together again, that Satan tempt you not for your incontinency.

Carefully notice these points from the Word of God:

- The best way to avoid fornication (and adultery) is a good marriage.

- Benevolence (kindly understanding) is to be practiced between husband and wife in sex.

- Withholding sex from one another is *defrauding* each other. It's both wrong and incompatible with a scriptural married life, except for a mutually agreed on period of fasting and prayer (doing this together), and then resuming harmonious sex together again. This is for a most important reason: to prevent satan from tempting either or both to be drawn sexually to someone outside their marriage.

The lack of the Church's teaching on this all-important subject and function was very hurtful. So I studied the Bible for myself and worked out with my wife God's ordained way for us to be "fruitful" as well as to "multiply."

Evelyn and I discovered that one or two talks about sex are not enough. Having an openness to discuss it any time has saved us much resentment and lack of closeness.

Also being affectionate both openly and in private contributes much to a normal, happy sex life.

With due respect to my parents, we children never saw them hug each other or kiss or show any outward affection in our presence.

They managed to have a good marriage for 66 years. We knew they loved each other. However, it would have meant so much more had we seen them affectionate to each other.

Some people view affection as wrong. I think it is out of place only if it is a put-on and not carried over into the bedroom and the rest of life. One of the highest compliments many people have given Evelyn and me is on the sincere and unabashed affection we have shown to each other.

The fact is, both of us would be incomplete without showing affection to the other.

KEY #5

We read the Bible and pray together beyond our personal Bible study and prayer times.

This key has helped bind us closer together. It is an indispensable way to think in God's terms, rather than relying on our own understanding of life and of each other.

Fortunately, we're both readers and consistent students of God's Word, which we prize above all. We also read books, newspapers, national news magazines, and value certain programs on television, radio, CDs, and tapes.

Although we separate the spiritual from the profane, we do not separate the spiritual from the secular.

We respect the secular because all of us are both spiritual and secular in our makeup.

It is wisdom to understand we're not in Heaven yet. We should not be so heavenly minded we are of no earthly good. We are earthbound creatures until God calls us to our eternal home.

So our reading covers a great deal of life. The Bible, however, is our number one book, and books, tapes, etc., related to it.

As we study the Bible individually or together, Evelyn and I find ourselves being integrated in the Word both when we are in church and in our daily lives. This is our way of life.

KEY #6

Integrity of life and action is all-important in marriage.

Integrity was ingrained in me by my preacher-father, Reverend Ellis Melvin Roberts. Papa would never buy on credit unless it was the only way, the final way. He would not live with debt. Every dollar above his living expenses he paid on a debt until it was gone. Only then was he happy. He paid his bills strictly on time and often before! His credit was always good, although he seldom used it.

I must say he "ground" that into us children. Each one of us got it, believe me. To this day my total concern in financial matters of my ministry and personal life is to pay as I go. I have no debts if there is any way possible to avoid them.

God called me to build Him a major university. I refused to borrow money, started with no money, and built it just by God's command and faith. That included the City of Faith

Medical and Research Center. At a cost of almost $500 million, we opened all of it debt-free!

Only when offerings to God's work fell off dramatically in the late 1980s and early '90s, did I and many others suffer a loss and fall behind. Having to borrow money broke my heart. We've labored long and hard to overcome this terrible fallout in our finances.

Richard, my able son, who followed me as the second president and CEO of Oral Roberts University, has reduced the debt, and we expect to be completely out of debt again very soon. He has vowed *never to be in debt again*, and I'm in full Bible agreement with him. The Bible says, "Owe no man" (Rom. 13:8a). That's my credo, my integrity of not being "servant to the lender" (Prov. 22:7b). I want to have the apostle's integrity right up to the end. (See Second Timothy 4:7-8.)

My constant advice to ministers is, "Stay out of debt—in your marriage and in your ministry."

I understand there are certain situations when borrowing seems necessary, but in most cases you can *by your faith* pay as you go. If you're building a building for your ministry, people will respond far more than they will in paying off debt. If you're buying or building a home, or purchasing a new car, or buying anything else, remember God has given you faith to believe and save to secure these things altogether—or at least in substantial part—debt-free. You have to believe this in your heart, in your emotions, and always remember that God says throughout His Word, "The just shall live by faith" (see Hab. 2:4; Rom. 1:17).

Pay your bills! Be extra careful if using a credit card—save that ungodly interest! (I carry only one credit card, and I am careful *never* to spend more than I have in the bank on it.) Guard your integrity.

KEY #7

Morals and Christian behavior might be the most serious part of the marriage.

Evelyn and I thank God we can honestly testify of clean living. We believe if there is a trip-up, and it is faced quickly and squarely, it can be overcome. I do not believe God quickly forsakes anyone, and that most certainly includes not only His beloved ministers, but each of us. He cares that much about us.

Not everyone called into the ministry has had a completely moral life. Then why did God call them? I believe He has no one to call to preach His gospel who has no weaknesses, shortcomings, or failures. None of us was ever perfect, and we're not now. We are imperfect vessels. Fortunately, the majority of us are dedicated to God to the extent that we fight with our faith to be moral in every way, to keep our marriages and live an exemplary life.

If we see we have a tendency toward a certain weakness (we are all born with some form of weakness as a result of the fall of man and the curse of sin on man and the earth), we must honestly recognize and face that weakness. Instead of having the attitude, "I was born with this, and there's nothing I can do about it," we can face it

- with utter dependence on God,

- with our will and purpose,

- with prayer and faith,

- and with the right kind of pride which Joseph in the Old Testament had. For example:

When Joseph refused the invitation of Potiphar's wife in Egypt to commit adultery with her, he said, "I will not sin against God by doing this," and fled despite her false accusations.

In spite of being thrown into jail, Joseph knew he was innocent. He eventually won out, as we all will, if we follow his example. (See Genesis 39:7-15.)

Admittedly, more is expected of ministers. There is less sympathy if we fail or fall, but why not? We represent the high calling of God. We preach the greatest gospel, the very power of God to save, heal, and change the world. Satan's greatest desire and effort is to get into the minds and emotions of ministers. He tries to seduce them in areas of their inborn weaknesses, particularly the inclination to commit immoral acts and rebel against God. Then he tries to convince them that their sin won't harm their marriage or ministry.

The apostle Peter tells us, "Be sober, be vigilant; because your adversary the devil, as a roaring lion, walketh about, seeking whom he may devour" (1 Pet. 5:8).

When I entered marriage with Evelyn, she said, "Oral, when we marry, that's it. There'll be no divorce in this family."

She was speaking my language. A child of divorce herself, she had suffered because of it.

She'd made up her mind that divorce would not touch her marriage. I grew up under parents to whom divorce did not exist. They lived together 66 years, committed to each other, and produced five children.

I had seen divorce almost wreck the life of my sister Jewel. When she was very young she had run off and married a handsome guy who turned out to be an escaped convict. Billie June, the one child of that union, was raised mostly by my parents.

After Jewel's conversion, her second marriage lasted 60 years and was blessed in every way. She and her husband had two daughters who, when grown, became women of God.

As a young preacher, I was bitter against divorce, taking the *letter* of the Bible rather than the *spirit* of God's Word.

Later, I found you cannot connect with people in their weaknesses by putting the letter of the Bible above compassion. This can cause untold dangers.

Some ministers have divorce as the main theme of their preaching, only to have divorce enter their family in some way. I learned to be wary of preachers who harp on one or two types of sin or shortcomings. I'm suspicious of them.

It is better to stick with the "whole counsel of God" (see Acts 20:27) and harmonize one Scripture with the rest of the Bible (see Lk. 24:27).

As Evelyn says so often, "Marriage is not something you jump into with the idea if everything doesn't go right, you can jump right out and look for another. God must be taken into consideration: What does He say?"

There may be that rare occasion when a terrible mistake is made to begin with. Peace and harmony become impossible, and the marriage breaks up. If another marriage is sought, each must go back to God's basic principles for a right marriage, a successful marriage, a lasting marriage. Just stop and remember, God can make your marriage work if you work with Him.

After 63 years of a happy, fruitful marriage, I want to emphasize the key issue to every young single or newlywed who desires similar precious results. The bottom line is that you must both know in your heart of hearts that God is in your marriage. You must be and do your part. At the same time look to God as your Source, ask for His help by sowing your seeds of faith continually, and learn to depend on Him as your Source to work things out in you and for you.

Then you will have a truly successful marriage. Not only will you be blessed, but you and your children will bless others because of your witness for the Lord.

Depending on the Lord has certainly worked for Evelyn and me in the ups and downs, the attacks of satan on us or our children, and for staying the course in a marriage we both know was joined by and ordered of the Lord. To this day, we love and adore each other. Through our love and our growing together as one, we try above all things to continuously trust God as our Source, as well as our personal Savior and Lord.

Evelyn is my dear, sweet wife. I believe in her, I trust her, I live with her under God's laws, and I expect to until God calls me home.

Marriage and family are our most precious gifts. My slogan for it is

It

can

Be Done.

IMPORTANT POINTS

1. Let God lead you to your spouse-to-be.

2. Have in mind to marry for life.

3. Being opposites in temperament can be an integral part of your marriage success.

4. Practicing a good sex life in marriage is connected closely to your spiritual development.

5. Read the Bible and pray *together* over and beyond your personal Bible study and prayer times.

6. Integrity of life and action is all-important in marriage and in life.

7. Morals and Christian behavior might be the most serious part of the marriage to be faced and followed.

8. You can have a good, solid marriage. Your faith is the key.

12

How I Saw the Invisible in the Delayed Birth of My Son Richard

I happened this way. By a consensus of the sponsoring pastors of my first Dallas, Texas, crusade in November 1948 and the agreement of faith between Evelyn and me, our son Richard's birth was delayed two days, and at a specific deadline that goes beyond explanation by human factors.

The crusade was scheduled for 16 days. Each night the crusade tent quickly filled up, with hundreds standing all around the outside. By raising the side curtain, we could handle several thousand more people.

By the final day the crusade was stirring the city, jammed with record crowds, and the results before our eyes were truly astonishing. God was moving. The pastors met me the afternoon before the closing service and asked me to continue the crusade three more days.

"Brethren," I said, "my wife is in Tulsa scheduled to give birth to our third child next Wednesday. I am duty bound to drive home after tonight's service, take a couple days of rest, and be with her on Wednesday when the baby is due."

"We understand that," the chairman said. "But if you could give us just three more days, we believe more than a thousand more souls will be saved, besides large numbers receiving their healing from the hand of the Lord. Can't you and your wife postpone your baby's birth in order for this to happen?"

"Postpone the baby's birth!" I exclaimed. "The doctor set the date months ago. Evelyn feels the movement of the baby in her body is right on schedule. How could we postpone it?"

The pastors were dead serious. We faced a great problem. Everyone was quiet, but I could feel something inside me I had never felt before. The chairman said, "We've met and prayed about this. Never before have we had a crusade like this. Our churches are being revived, the city is stirred, the crusade is at its peak.

"How can we see it close? Isn't God, who sent you here and gave all these supernatural results, able to intervene in Tulsa and cause the baby to be born a few days after Wednesday?"

One pastor spoke up and said, "Brother Oral, would you be willing to phone your wife and ask her to postpone the baby's birth beyond Wednesday?"

Talk about seeing the invisible! All kinds of thoughts went through my mind. While I am part Cherokee Indian, Evelyn is a full-blooded German, highly organized and methodical. *She has everything ready for this birth. What is she going to say if I call her to do this?*

I said, "Let's join hands and pray, each of us praying one after the other."

For the next several minutes we had a fervent prayer, and with tears. When the prayers ended, faces were glowing with

God's presence. A strange peace settled over my spirit as the group laid hands on me and prayed, "God, let our brother see." I was beginning to see beyond the natural.

"All right," I said, "I'll phone Evelyn." As they stood by, I reached Evelyn, and the moment she picked up the phone I dumped the whole thing on her.

Predictably, she said, "Oral, are you out of your mind? I can't tell this baby when to be born. Our doctor has just examined me and said the baby, according to all signs, is right on time. What are you asking me to do?"

"It's not me, darling, asking you," I said. "We've got to measure the pastors' request, think of possibly saving more than a thousand more souls, besides the many who will be healed."

"Well, Oral, what are you proposing?"

"Evelyn, we're called of God. We're committed to Him. His hand is on us, and He's doing something extraordinary in this crusade. Naturally I want to come home tonight after the services and be with you for the baby's birth Wednesday. What I'm proposing is an act of faith for both of us to see beyond Wednesday the birth of our baby."

"And that is?"

"Come into agreement by faith that God will intervene and *do the impossible* by letting you have the baby a little late."

There was silence on the other end of the phone. Then, "All right, Oral. If you will pray with me over the phone, I'll agree that God will postpone the birth until Friday night and that the baby will be born by midnight."

She added, "But I want your word you'll drive home after the service Wednesday night."

I agreed.

When the announcement was made in the Sunday night service that the crusade would be extended three more days, there was enthusiastic applause. I made no mention of praying for the postponement of my child's birth beyond the appointed time.

Well, those three days exceeded anything we had seen the previous sixteen days in the crusade—overflowing crowds, spectacular miracles of healing, and far more than a thousand souls saved. I was 30 years old and only in the second year of my healing ministry, but I felt as David said in the Bible that "I could run through a troop and jump over a wall" (see 2 Sam. 22:30). Honestly, I felt both humbled and as tall as a mountain in my faith.

I arrived home at 3 a.m. Thursday and fell into the bed beside my darling wife.

On Friday evening we had dinner guests. After the meal, Evelyn got up, picked up the bag she had packed, and said, "Oral, it's time to go to the hospital. Our baby is due to be born before midnight." By this time we had a peace about it. She too had seen the invisible.

When the attending nurse examined Evelyn, she said, "Dearie, you may as well take your bag and go home. You're not going to have this baby tonight, and I'm not going to call the doctor to come."

Evelyn said, "Nurse, my baby will be born before midnight. You'd better get the doctor here."

Turning away, the nurse said, "No, dearie, no baby tonight. Besides, by this time the doctor is in bed. I'm not calling him. Go home."

I saw that look on Evelyn's face. "Okay, nurse. Remember I told you that this baby will be here before midnight. You'd better call the doctor." The nurse was unmoved.

Evelyn turned to me. "Honey, why don't you go out into the waiting room? I'll send word when the baby is arriving."

The room was filled with other fathers-to-be. I had brought my writing materials, as I was working on a new book. Soon I was absorbed in my writing when a young man leaned over and said, "Writing, huh?" I nodded.

"Writing a book?"

"Yes."

"What kind of book?"

"About faith."

"Who are you?"

"My name is Roberts."

"Oral Roberts?"

"Yes."

He jumped up and grabbed my shoulder. "Oral Roberts, I've been here two days and nights waiting for my wife to have our baby. She's been told not to go home, but they don't know exactly when the baby will come."

He was haggard looking and greatly distressed. "Stay right here," he said, and disappeared down the hallway.

Soon he returned with his young wife. She looked at me and said, "Are you Oral Roberts?"

"Yes, I am."

"In person?"

"Yes, I'm in person."

"Oh, Oral Roberts," she cried, "all the pains are on me but my baby just won't come. Will you pray for me?"

I put my writing aside, stood up, and said, "Let me have your right hand."

By this time her face was flooded with tears. I said, "Look at me a moment and listen with your inner self." She nodded her head that she would.

"The Bible says in First Timothy 2:15 that you shall be saved in childbearing. The apostle Paul said that the Lord is more concerned that your baby will be born than you are. You are a child of God, aren't you?"

"Oh, yes," she said.

"All right. Let's pray."

Afterwards I said, "Now you go in there and have that baby. Do you hear me?"

"Yes," she said, "I'll do it." Looking at her husband, she said, "I feel the baby coming now. It will be here soon." And she hurried away.

Meanwhile Evelyn came out into the waiting room and said, "Oral, walk with me up and down the hall and pray with me. They say the baby is not going to be born until in the morning. But we agreed that the Lord would cause it to be born before midnight."

I took her arm and we began walking the halls, holding to our agreement we had made over the phone. In minutes Evelyn's contractions began—strong. The nurse went into action.

Putting Evelyn on a gurney, she rolled her into the delivery room. On the way there, we saw the girl with whom I had prayed being wheeled out of the delivery room. As she passed Evelyn, she said, "I beat you."

At twenty minutes before midnight Richard Lee Roberts was born, his little fists clenched as if to say, "Here I come! I'm ready to take on the world."

I believe the birth of Richard had a supernatural element (not that he was a supernatural child—only the holy child Jesus was supernaturally born).

Looking at Richard's anointed ministry of healing and as the president and CEO of Oral Roberts University, I marvel at the way God is healing the sick through him and causing ORU to go beyond my own efforts. I often recall the supernaturalness surrounding his birth—how his mother and I saw the invisible and watched the impossible happen.

We had four children—Rebecca, Ronnie, Richard, and Roberta—in that order. All are special to us. All became strong Christians.

IMPORTANT POINTS

1. God said, "Things which are seen were not made of things which do appear" (Heb. 11:3b).

2. You can come into agreement by faith to see the invisible, which enables you to do the impossible.

3. Seeing the invisible and doing the impossible has happened to me, and to others of faith, many times. It can happen to you.

13

How I Learned Ten Principles for Handling My Personal and Ministry Finances

My consultant for this chapter has been my esteemed friend, Robert W. Katz, CPA. Robert was healed through my television ministry at age four, and was converted to Jesus in his early twenties.

He furnished me much of the technical material, which helped me put my personal experiences and thoughts together on finances, an integral part of everyone's life and ministry. This chapter is what I try to live by every day of my life.

In this chapter we will discuss key principles for successfully handling both our personal and ministry finances and our responsibilities as stewards over the Lord's tithes, offerings, and alms.

Why is this so important to study and know? One of the most common ways satan causes ministers to stumble is to entice them to mismanage their *personal finances* and the *finances of their church or ministry*. According to my study of the Bible, spirits of lack, poverty, and greed roam the earth pitting husband against wife, children against parents, and even shepherds against their sheep. As a result, marriages fail, relationships crumble, and ministries are destroyed.

The good news, however, is that the greatest book ever written on stewardship is in our hands. The Bible provides us with a poignant five thousand-year history of man's struggles with stewardship and provides relevant answers to every *financial* question you and I will ever encounter.

Over two thousand verses in Scripture, as well as two-thirds of the parables, reveal lessons to us about finances and stewardship. They show us how to see the invisible and do the impossible financially.

God uses the spiritual to teach us about the material and the supernatural to teach us about the natural.

You may ask, "But why would the Lord use the supernatural to teach about our finances?"

He looks deep into our hearts and knows, "Where your treasure is, there your heart will be also" (Mt. 6:21 NIV). If we mismanage what the Lord has entrusted to us; if our personal finances are a mess; then our work will also be in bondage. I've seen this happen when preachers and other believers never intended it to happen. And I've made mistakes of my own.

I'm sharing with you what I've learned, and am still learning—the down-to-earth basics of biblical stewardship and responsibility for our work and our personal finances before our God. In this chapter I will discuss ten principles I have used to help govern my finances in my personal life and ministry.

PRINCIPLE #1—Start at the beginning of financial wisdom.

Will a man rob God? Yet you rob Me. But you ask, "How do we rob You?" In tithes and offerings. You are under a curse—the whole nation of you— because you are robbing Me (Malachi 3:8-9 NIV).

The best poll available uncovered the incredible fact that only 32 percent of pastors tithe! That's less than two-thirds! The very basic beginning of financial wisdom is when we get into the spirit of giving—with joy and expectation.

We must teach and practice God's giving and receiving principle—Seed-Faith! Better still, practice Seed-Faith, then teach it. I've found that God's people are hungry to know how to practice Seed-Faith when they learn it is the core teaching of the Bible on seedtime and harvest. (See Genesis 8:22.) (Be sure you read Chapter 18 about Seed-Faith. It can transform your life!)

If my ministry and yours do not continually plant the *seeds* of tithes, offerings, and helping the unfortunate, then we will never reap the miracle harvests that the Lord intended for our lives and for our ministries. Never!

A rejected (or neglected) opportunity to sow seeds of faith is a lost opportunity to receive a miracle harvest, which includes financial harvests.

We see from Abram's example in Genesis 14:18-20 that our giving tithe is not an option. It is the earthly manifestation of the *seal of our faith*. God says, "The just shall live by faith" (Rom. 1:17).

God's spiritual laws

    of sowing and reaping,

        of seedtime and harvest,

            of giving and receiving are all predicated on our faith.

119

As for me, once I saw this I realized we *gain* the blessing of Abraham by tithing and we grow by giving. From Hebrews 7, we know that Melchizedek is a type of Jesus. When our seed is sown, it is sown directly into the hands of Jesus. I have been faithful to give tithes of all my finances, as my Seed-Faith. Receiving *the* blessing—not just a blessing—has made all the difference in my life and ministry. I believe it will do the same for your faith, and will positively change your entire finances for you personally, and in doing God's work.

It's true that you can gain without following the Bible principles of giving and receiving, of sowing and reaping. But in the final analysis, your wallet will still have holes in it. Your ministry will fall short and dishonor God and yourself.

If I ignore the Scripture's instruction regarding sowing my tithes and offerings to the Lord's work, and expectantly look for the specific promise of *God's miracle returns*, most of my financial miracle returns will pass me by. I am convinced the same thing will happen to you. As I continue to learn about Seed-Faith, I recommend it as the pattern for life and ministry.

PRINCIPLE #2—You are held to a higher standard by God and man.

> *...From everyone who has been given much, much will be demanded; and from the one who has been entrusted with much, much more will be asked* (Luke 12:48 NIV).

Because you are in the Lord's work, in all of your financial dealings, you must—*you must*—accept the fact that you will be held to a higher standard by both man and God. You must avoid at all cost financial dilemmas that others commonly experience (such as going deeply into debt or making unwise investment decisions).

> You and I must live our financial lives as if every day the local newspaper printed a copy of our personal financial statements and checkbook on its front page.

This may seem to be a hard teaching. But only to the degree that we can handle financial matters, will the Lord let us handle spiritual matters. In Luke 16:1-13 Jesus makes it clear that our stewardship of money is related to the Lord's trusting us with the "true riches" of spiritual things. If we mismanage what the Lord has entrusted to us, the ministry will lose its anointing, in the same way that King Saul lost his anointing. (See First Samuel 15, which is appropriately titled, "The Lord Rejects Saul as King.")

Leviticus 27:30 NIV tells us that the tithe is "holy to the Lord"; therefore, our oversight of it is a sacred trust. It is imperative that every penny collected be used for the purpose for which it was intended. We must not take up a collection for missions and then use it for other purposes. It is a sacred trust, and God will honor us for keeping it sacred.

Don't touch the gold!

Why then did you not obey the voice of the Lord?
Why did you swoop down on the spoil, and do evil
in the sight of the Lord? (1 Samuel 15:19 NKJV).

Finally, God showed me that I must never violate His principle as Ananias and Sapphira did. Their mishandling of finances and subsequent deceit had disastrous consequences. (See Acts 5:1-10.)We must not allow our hands to take anything of the Lord's that was not intended for us. If we do, we will bring reproach on ourselves, our ministries, and our families.

121

And remember, there is the Internal Revenue Service watching over our shoulders. You and I are to do everything openly and aboveboard financially.

We are called not just to be preachers but shepherds, and a shepherd leads by example. One of the most common problems for which our flock will seek Bible counsel is financial difficulties. We are their mentors. If our own financial house is not in order, our counseling will not have God's anointing upon it.

If our congregation cannot trust our judgment with worldly possessions, how can they trust our judgment in spiritual matters? Fortunately, I saw this correlation early in my ministry. I give God credit for the fact there's never been a financial scandal attached to my personal life and my ministry.

The Lord holds ministers and Christian businesspeople to a high standard. He has entrusted *us* with His most precious possession, His children. It is awesome to know that we will be held accountable for how well we have led and taught them. Scripture warns, "Not many of you should presume to be teachers, my brothers, because you know that we who teach will be judged more strictly" (Jas. 3:1 NIV).

PRINCIPLE #3—Seek Godly wisdom in handling money.

God's Word says, "Get wisdom, get understanding; do not forget my words or swerve from them. Do not forsake wisdom, and she will protect you; love her, and she will watch over you. Wisdom is supreme; therefore get wisdom..." (Prov. 4:5-7 NIV).

I have heard that 90 percent of pastors report that they were not properly prepared to take on the responsibilities of ministry. I suspect that an equal number of us would say that we were not properly prepared to handle the responsibilities of our personal finances, let alone the finances of our church or ministry. I know it was true in my life.

These responsibilities are extremely complicated, and few of us, inside or outside of the ministry, have ever been formally trained to assume them. What do you do? Here are three suggestions:

Number 1. First, heed the warning of the prophet Hosea, "My people are destroyed for lack of knowledge" (Hos. 4:6).

Early on I accepted the fact that I would be facing financial issues all my life. In my college work, I took courses in finance. At my local Christian bookstore I found excellent books on Christian financial planning and church financial management. I urge you to buy several of these types of books and to continually refer to them.

Number 2. Next, very cautiously and very carefully begin to surround yourself with counselors.

The Body of Christ has many members who can provide you with wise counsel. Ask the Lord to bless you with men and women of godly wisdom and influence who will provide you with helpful counsel in matters of stewardship. Sometimes it is wise to go to secular financial advisors.

Number 3. Finally, remember that every question you encounter regarding stewardship is answered in Scripture.

There are no new questions. Ecclesiastes 1:9 NIV reminds us that, "What has been will be again, what has been done will be done again; there is nothing new under the sun."

I earnestly made it a priority to seek the Lord for supernatural wisdom, and soon I found He was providing it. I did not have to remain ignorant of financial knowledge. Much help was available, if only I sought it.

For instance, you may be approached by a nonbeliever who wants you to join in a business venture that holds great promise for profit. However, after prayer, and thorough checking, the Lord will reveal to you, "Do not be yoked together with unbelievers" (2 Cor. 6:14a NIV). This also includes not being unequally yoked with believers who sometimes come up with schemes of their own.

You can count on the Lord supernaturally revealing His counsel in these matters if you pray and use common sense. I know of several young ministers who got caught up in "deals" offered them. So far I have refused all such deals. I would rather sow my seeds of faith and trust *God my Source* for my miracle harvests.

PRINCIPLE #4—Seek God and His spiritual prosperity and you will be in a position to have no lack.

And my God will meet all your needs according to His glorious riches in Christ Jesus (Philippians 4:19 NIV).

Throughout the first 12 years of my ministry I suffered much material lack because my denomination taught the poverty concept, much of which remains in the Body of Christ today. I saw God's prosperity for His children in His Word. I chose to believe *God is a good God*. Many people saw this revelation in the Bible, but they rejected it out of fear of criticism. They actually dug their own financial grave.

I remember being called before the official leaders of a powerful denomination who attacked me on Seed-Faith. They said I was not preaching the Bible. I handed them my Bible and said, "Show me." They couldn't do it, and we stared at each other in our impasse.

They were honestly speaking out of their poverty concept, and I was honestly speaking out of the eternal principle of seedtime and harvest. The Lord came into our midst and broke us up inside; we began a wonderful fellowship which lasts to this day.

God wants us to succeed in every area of our lives, including our finances, in order to do His work worldwide. *This is based first on our needs being met.*

Over and over this Scripture moved me: "Do not let this Book of the Law depart from your mouth; meditate on it day and night, so that you may be careful to do everything written in it. Then you will be *prosperous and successful*" (Josh. 1:8 NIV).

God's prosperity for each of us is *having more than enough* to do what the Lord has called us to do. If our heart is truly in sowing and reaping, God will absolutely meet *all* our needs according to His riches (not man's alone) in glory. (See Galatians 6:7; Philippians 4:19; Matthew 17:20.)

When this truth entered my spirit, I began looking at my needs in an entirely different light—no longer as satan's advantage over me, but as my opportunity to move deeper into sowing my seeds of faith and expecting God's "due season" where I would reap my miracle harvests (see Gal. 6:9).

This is my lifestyle personally and in my ministry, the pattern of my whole life. I'm not influenced by critics who are blind to the promise of God's prosperity for His own. He wants us to witness to all nations so the end can come. (See Matthew 24:14.)

Misfortune pursues the sinner, but prosperity is the reward of the righteous (Proverbs 13:21 NIV).

Be not deceived; God is not mocked: for whatsoever a man soweth, that shall he also reap (Galatians 6:7).

125

PRINCIPLE #5—Take care of your family's financial needs.

[We] *must manage our* [own] *family well...(If anyone does not know how to manage his own family, how can he take care of God's church?)* (1 Timothy 3:4-5 NIV).

God's order of priority is that He put the family first, even before He established the Church. So your ministry is in close relationship to your family. They are to come first in your financial responsibility.

If you neglect your family, you are planting seeds of resentment. Yes, we can plant bad seeds, which bring bad harvests. I have heard stories of many embittered pastors' wives who believe that all they receive are the scraps, financial and otherwise, left over after all has been given to the ministry. I have heard many stories of children growing up resentful that they were never properly provided for because of the ministry. As a preacher's kid, I was one of these. Lack of finances was the chief reason I ran away from home at an early age.

Ministry poverty is not a badge of courage, nor is it a light to a lost and dying world.

I should know. After I began my ministry, I did not put my family first, and sadly I reaped a bad harvest until with my wife's help I saw the light in the Word of God.

Finally I saw it was my responsibility to properly manage my family's finances. I saw that this responsibility is not just a matter of simply paying my bills. *It is having a financial plan.* This plan should address the various financial situations you will encounter at different stages in your life.

I began to realize my faith included giving thoughtful and prayerful consideration to matters such as financial emergencies, insurance needs, buying a home (yes, every preacher should own his own home—debt-free!), investing, the cost of my children's higher education, retirement planning, and so forth. I saw if I didn't do it, no one else would. It was up to me and the Lord.

I recommend that you approach these concerns in a similar manner as described in Principle #3. Buy and study several good books on Christian financial planning for your family. Seek the advice of wise financial counselors. Sow seed that you "aim" at this need. You'll find that "the desires of the diligent are fully satisfied" (Prov. 13:4b NIV).

PRINCIPLE #6—Beware of debt.

The rich rule over the poor, and the borrower is servant to the lender (Proverbs 22:7 NIV).

I believe that in the United States, one of satan's greatest spiritual weapons against us is *fear*. His greatest natural weapon is getting us to go into debt that is over our faith and our common sense.

Talk about fear! Debt tends to fill us with fear that crushes and consumes. We're subject to the lender, with its interest and monthly payments, whether we have it or not. It can separate us from trusting a loving God and carrying out His true purpose for our lives. It is a many-tentacled monster that lives to wrap itself around us, pulling us under to a place where the pressure is so great we cannot breathe.

Listen to the outcry of the Israelites in Nehemiah:

We have had to borrow money to pay the king's tax on our fields and vineyards. Although we are of the same flesh and blood as our countrymen and though our sons are as good as theirs, yet we have to subject our sons and daughters to slavery. Some of our daughters have already been enslaved, but we are powerless, because our fields and our vineyards belong to others (Nehemiah 5:4b-5 NIV).

And then listen to the advice of Paul, "Let no debt remain outstanding, except the continuing debt to love one another" (Rom. 13:8a NIV). He must have had some bad experiences with debt.

The Lord's plan, from the very beginning, has always been, "The Lord your God will bless you as He has promised, and you will lend to many nations but will borrow from none. You will rule over many nations but none will rule over you" (Deut. 15:6 NIV).

I understand that there may be major purchases early in our career that will probably involve debt, specifically the purchase of a house or car. These are temporarily acceptable debts because the loans we make are associated with an asset of equal or greater value. That is, if necessary, we could sell our house or car and extinguish the debt upon it.

However, we should *never* take on a debt that is not associated with an asset, such as credit card debt, consolidation loans, credit union loans, or any of the other plentiful and readily obtainable "easy" credit. As soon as possible, your goal should be to *become and remain* debt-free.

If you feel you have to borrow for your ministry, it, too, should be associated with an asset, with direct guidance from the Lord. Many pastors are building new sanctuaries or additions by paying as they go. This has been my practice at Oral Roberts University. I suggest you confer with such leaders and learn how they're doing it. Others are borrowing only part and raising the balance as they build.

It is always wise to hear God's voice on the way *He* wants you to build. Once He shows you the invisible—the vision you are to fulfill in your life—He will *show you* how to do the impossible. I mean that literally.

I tell you out of hard personal experience: man will let you down. God is your only true Source. I practice saying to myself, *God is my Source!*

Above all, my advice is to get the mind of God 100 percent first; follow it wholeheartedly; and you'll never go wrong.

PRINCIPLE #7—Avoid schemes and dreams.

The first to present his case seems right, till another comes forward and questions him (Proverbs 18:17 NIV).

As I have been, you will be approached. Well-meaning and not so well-meaning people will come to you with potential investments.

And they will sound good.

My experience is to run from these financial dealings. If you participate in these deals, one of two things will happen. *The investment will do well and the relationship will be weakened because the adviser will believe that he is now entitled to a special influence over your life; or the investment will do poorly, hurting your relationship, even to losing precious friends.*

I've learned I am not to look to anyone else to provide wealth for me. We should look to God as our Source of provision. "Commit to the Lord whatever you do, and your plans will succeed" (Prov. 16:3 NIV). Again I say, God is your Source, not man.

PRINCIPLE #8—Find someone to whom you will be accountable.

Remember the Roman captain who said to Jesus, "For I myself am a man under authority, with soldiers under me. I tell this one, 'Go,' and he goes; and that one, 'Come,' and he comes. I say to my servant, 'Do this,' and he does it" (Matthew 8:9 NIV).

It is the Lord's plan for us to be accountable to someone who is spiritually more mature than we, and where possible, someone who is better disciplined financially.

Prayerfully seek the Lord to lead you to someone whose character and integrity are beyond reproach, someone who can be a careful and wise counselor and advisor to you. And when the Lord has identified that person to you, consider taking suggestions from them concerning your ministry and your personal life (finances included).

Reveal your strengths and weaknesses and set long- and short-term goals that you can jointly monitor. I discovered this is not an easy person to locate. I say, "Careful. Careful."

In addition to the spiritual and financial leader to whom you may be accountable, share your financial decisions with your spouse. God has given you a spouse to make you whole.

Besides, your spouse lives with you as your life's partner. It was several years into our marriage before Evelyn and I acted as one in all our financial decisions. I wish we had done this earlier. It is so important.

Without their wife's intuitive nature and sense of discernment, men sometimes make financial decisions that may not receive their full anointing. The men are using only half of the reasoning power that the Lord has made available to them.

PRINCIPLE #9—Surprise: Your success will be harder to handle than your failure.

The ground of a certain rich man produced a good crop....Then he said, "This is what I'll do. I will tear down my barns and build bigger ones, and there I will store all my grain and my goods. And I'll say to myself, 'You have plenty of good things laid up for many years. Take life easy; eat, drink and be merry.' " But God said to him, "You fool! This very night your life will be demanded from you..." (Luke 12:16b-20 NIV).

I came under much more pressure when success came to me and to my ministry. It was a whole new ballgame—with entirely new rules and responsibility.

Solomon, the richest and most successful man ever to live, uses the term "meaningless" no fewer than 31 times as he laments about his life in the Book of Ecclesiastes. For him the struggles of youth had brought great obedience and focus. But he allowed the success of maturity only to bring him great distraction and ruin. It is a powerful lesson to us to remain vigilant.

- As we submit ourselves to the Lord,

- pursue Him with our whole heart,

- and seek His guidance and wisdom, then we *will succeed.*

It is precisely at that moment of success that we will need to be the most submitted to the Lord and to our calling.

Be careful when you want to buy everything you never had or ever wanted.

Beware when you begin to think that you can't fail.

Watch when your personal walk with God grows stale and your secret place with Him is abandoned. It is at that hour that you have brought yourself to the precipice of greatest peril.

I remember how I fought this. I made some mistakes I rue to this day, and they were all my fault. I couldn't handle success very well at first. For this reason, I can share with you.

Satan is always one step behind you. He will urge you to touch the tithe, or to borrow it. To covet someone else's gifts. To sell your birthright for a quick reward. If you do these things, it is all over, as Esau learned (see Gen. 27:30-38; Heb. 12:17).

An addiction, adultery, a mishandling of money, or an attitude and acts of arrogance can destroy us. These can be overcome.

It will require confession,

> humility you've not known before,

>> and time (yes, time) to reach a place where you can have a new beginning.

Remember the old adage, "An ounce of prevention is worth a pound of cure." This is true in the lives and ministries of preachers and others.

All of you, clothe yourselves with humility toward one another, because, "God opposes the proud but gives grace to the humble" (1 Peter 5:5 NIV).

PRINCIPLE #10—Be sure to take care of the Lord's business, and He will be sure to take care of yours.

And without faith it is impossible to please God, because anyone who comes to Him must believe that He exists and that He rewards those who earnestly seek Him (Hebrews 11:6 NIV).

Stewardship, as the Lord intends, will always be a *faith walk*. Always. I once asked God to define faith to me. His answer changed my life. He said, "Faith is when the Holy Spirit supernaturally empties you of doubt, and fills you with a knowing, so in that moment you cannot doubt!"

You can step out in faith and reach your potential as God has called you. You can become so faith-conscious that a *knowing* will enter your spirit. In my experience, when the *knowing* is there, I cannot doubt. Miracles happen.

Making our faith as a seed we sow is what Jesus told His disciples in Matthew 17:20. They asked Him about their failures. He replied, "Because of your unbelief: for verily I say unto you, If ye have faith as a grain of mustard seed, ye shall say unto this mountain, Remove hence to yonder place; and it shall remove; and nothing shall be impossible unto you."

Why is this? It is because the action of our faith is like the action of a seed. Working your faith as a seed sown enables you to take care of God's work, and He will be sure to take care of yours.

The story is told that when the dirt covered the seed, it said to the seed, "I've got you covered now."

The seed replied, "No, you haven't. I'll grow right through you, no matter how heavy you are. I have the life of God in me."

And it did, growing and growing, producing and producing, and bringing great increase. The life of God is in the seeds you plant. I tell you from the bottom of my heart, Seed-Faith is the way I call my faith forth. It gives me a *knowing* He will take care of my finances, as well as the rest of my life, and enable me to be debt-free in my final years.

My prayer is that one or more of these ten principles concerning your personal and ministry finances will go deep into your heart. If so, I assure you, your better days are ahead.

IMPORTANT POINTS

1. Start at the beginning of financial wisdom.

2. You are held to a high standard by God and man.

3. Seek godly wisdom in handling money.

4. Seek God and His spiritual prosperity and you will be in a position to have no lack.

5. Take care of your family's financial needs.

6. Beware of debt.

7. Avoid schemes and dreams.

8. Find someone to whom you will be accountable.

9. Surprise: Your success will be harder to handle than your failure.

10. Be sure to take care of the Lord's business, and He will be sure to take care of yours.

14

HOW I LEARNED THE COST
OF OBEDIENCE IN THE MIDST
OF CONTROVERSY

n 1977 God commanded me to build the City of Faith Medical and Research Center for the purpose of *merging His healing streams of prayer and medicine.*

There was a hullabaloo by the medical world, the news media, and the average person on the street, that a healing evangelist would attempt such a thing—I was proposing a huge 2,200,000-square-foot complex.

The idea of merging prayer and medical science had been talked about many times but nobody had done anything major about it.

From the time I began my healing ministry in May 1947, I saw the healing power of prayer coming forth from my ministry of teaching, preaching, and healing. (See Matthew 4:23.) I also strongly believed that God healed by medicine, nutrition, exercise, positive thinking, and sometimes by climate.

I was soon saying these things to the crowds who thronged my crusades, but it was like I was talking into a vacuum. It was all invisible to them. By my faith I had seen the invisible; I knew in my spirit that I could do the impossible in bringing God's healing streams together. But it was a long, difficult road ahead.

Many times the sponsoring pastors of my crusades were from denominations that believed in healing by faith but in many instances were negative toward medicine. I didn't buy that. My parents, who prayed for the sick, were equally open to medical care. I grew up without prejudice toward either.

As I moved across America doing what I had been called to do—teaching, preaching, and laying hands on the sick—I was careful to state I could not heal, that only God could heal. I publicly urged those who believed they were healed through my prayers to return to their doctor for a checkup before they gave a testimony of healing. A raging controversy ensued, for which I was not prepared.

Church leaders often forbad their people to attend the crusades, only to see them come anyway in their desire for God to heal them. Some of the leadership of the denominations cooperated with the doubting and mocking stand the news media took everywhere.

There was no letup of the opposition. It just never quit. Yet the whole theory was in the Bible. I had to either turn to *God as my Source* as never before, or fold the big 10,000-seat tent cathedral and go home.

Early in my ministry I had vowed never to touch the gold or the glory and *never to strike back at my critics.*

I threw my whole life into obeying God, taking His healing power to my generation.

In 1954 I went on national television direct from the big tent, giving millions a front-row seat to see God heal and the opportunity to accept Christ as their personal Savior. This was the first time anything like this had been done. It was a big step for me—and for the nation.

Later, in God's time, we built Oral Roberts University—a university based on His authority and on the Holy Spirit. Today it is a fully accredited university—one of academics, aerobics, and spiritual excellence—sitting on a four hundred-acre campus in my home city, Tulsa.

The first buildings of Oral Roberts University opened officially in 1965. In the late '70s God's time came for me to open a medical school in ORU and build the massive City of Faith. I still had deep in my heart and emotions God's command—to take His healing power to my generation by merging His two main healing streams of prayer and medicine. This was not only because He wanted people to know that all healing is from Him, but also because He wanted the sick to be cured/healed—restored in their *whole person.*

That is the *key issue.* It was in Jesus' ministry; it is in ours today.

There was no effort from medical leaders and most church leaders to recognize that neither prayer nor medicine existed for itself, that neither was enough. The sick were not merely ill physically or spiritually. Many were sick in their total being.

They needed the best of prayer and the best of medicine interchangeably.

Being out there with thousands of desperately ill people in every crusade, I came face-to-face with this in a critical way.

I longed to see the merging, but I didn't see myself in position to bring it about. But God did. He spoke to me in that clear, familiar voice I had heard before and commanded me to take a major step to bring His healing streams together under one roof.

As had been my custom from the beginning of my ministry, I listened, prayed, and meditated on what God had said. I studied my Bible to see how what I had heard agreed with God's written Word. I saw it clearly in the Word of God as prophets, apostles, and other believers came face-to-face with the sick and deprived. (Luke, author of the Books of Luke and Acts, was a physician himself—see Colossians 4:14.) When I saw it in my spirit, as well as face-to-face with the multitudes, I waited for God's time to begin.

Count the Cost

I had already counted the cost of obedience to God's call on my life. Sometimes it became almost more than I could bear, to be vilified by some of the so-called top religious leaders, and to be constantly held up to ridicule and sensationalism by a news media that never took me out of their sights.

Knowing my Bible, I knew that obeying God was far greater than any misunderstanding and opposition that either satan or man could throw at me.

I had to obey God, no matter the cost.

The prophet Samuel said, "To obey is better than sacrifice, and to hearken than the fat of rams" (1 Sam. 15:22b). David left the testimony that he had "served his generation" (see Acts 13:36) and obeyed God, and Abraham "by faith... obeyed" (Heb. 11:8).

To keep focused and in unswerving obedience was the *key issue* to me. Survive or perish, I was set on obeying God.

138

When we announced in 1977 that ORU was going to build the medical school and City of Faith, the local medical establishment fought against us.

The gauntlet had been thrown down. It was me, a lone healing evangelist, against the entire opposition. But God always has had a *remnant*, a group who will not bow their knees to anyone except Him.

I discovered this remnant existed in every generation. The Bible bears out the fact that when God called someone to do a work for Him, He spoke in the hearts of certain people to *help*. He knew no one person could do the job, however willing he or she was. It was that way with me.

In early 1977 Evelyn, Richard, and I went to a place in one of the southwestern deserts to pray. There God spoke to me again and said, "I will rain on your desert." In His message to me, He gave me the invisible details for how to open the medical school and do the impossible in building the City of Faith. It was to be a medical/prayer complex with three towers—60, 30, and 20 stories *on one base*. In that massive complex we would begin merging His healing streams.

The very audacity of my building this complex and the immensity of the project captured the attention of the world, including such opposition as I had not anticipated or experienced before.

Because the medical community did not want the City of Faith, we were taken to court in Tulsa—and won; to the Oklahoma Supreme Court—and won. Four hundred thousand support letters from my Partner family poured into the Oklahoma legislature. Such a number of letters was unprecedented in the legislature's history. They promptly approved the project.

We had continued building during the trials and were about 20 stories up. The first $60 million of the final total of $180 million had come in and we had built debt-free so far.

The constant barrage of news stories and backstage oppositions had reached its peak. People were judging my efforts by what they read or heard in the news media.

The money stopped.

I refused to borrow.

We shut down.

If I couldn't complete the project as God said, *by faith*, it was not worth completing.

I admit my faith took a blow. I felt my faith was not as high as the skeleton-like shell of the building staring me in the face. "Oral's folly" was trumpeted everywhere. The media were having a field day. The medical establishment believed I could not complete it.

There was concern among the staff of Oral Roberts University and my evangelistic ministry team—not doubt or opposition, just concern, and much prayer. I practically lived in the Prayer Tower in the center of the campus. Two hundred feet up in that tower I have my special prayer room. I often spent time in fasting and prayer over the thousands of prayer requests sent by my Partners and others who were so ill or had other problems.

In spite of my faith, the world looked so dark. I hurt because I saw I was failing to carry out God's command. I knew I should not have felt that way, but I did.

Late one evening I parked just outside the chain-link fence surrounding the entire complex during the shutdown time. I stood by my car, one hand on top and the other reached out toward the unfinished giant of a building. As tears wet my face, I felt my heart would burst from my body. As I prayed, my whole body trembled. I felt a strong anointing.

The steel structure of the center building was over six hundred feet tall. It was to be the tallest building in Oklahoma. Suddenly by my spirit I saw Jesus appear, emerging from behind the building. I saw Him bend down and put His hands under the unfinished City of Faith structure and lift it. I heard Him say, "See how easy it is for Me to lift it?"

In a trembling voice I said, "Jesus! You can really lift it, can't You!"

He was Jesus Christ of Nazareth, the Son of the living God, before my spirit lifting the entire 2,200,000-square-foot structure of the City of Faith. And He was letting me know how easy it was for Him to lift it.

In sort of a strangled voice I cried, "Lord, we're running out of money again. The devil is trying to shut us down. He is trying to steal our Partners' support and our money flow."

Jesus said in a voice that seemed to fill my head and my whole body, "But I am not out of money. I own all the silver and gold in the earth. It was I who made Abraham rich in faith, in love, in vision, in money, so he would be the father of all who have faith."

Suddenly I thought of all the people of God who feel they are poor, and how sometimes all of us look at our billfolds and wonder when they will ever fill up.

As if Jesus were reading my thoughts, He said, "Neither you nor any of My children are poor except when you fail to know who God is, and who you are, then fail to give tithes of all as Abraham did. Now when you do this and give tithes of all as Seed-Faith to Me, My riches will flow to you to supply all your needs. I will put both the riches of Heaven *and* earth at the disposal of each of you who believe and obey Me, for I possess them both."

I said, "But, Jesus, I and my Partners have had faith for the first money and have obeyed in sending it in for the construction of the medical school and the City of Faith Medical Center this far. Now it seems I've brought it as far as I can." (This was the first time I felt I had used all the faith I had.)

As I kept looking at Jesus and thrilling at His magnificent presence before me, seeing how easy it was for Him to lift the City of Faith, He spoke to me again.

"Yes, this is as far as you can bring it. When I chose you to build it I told you that you could not build it by yourself, but that I would speak to your Partners and through them I would build it."

By this time I felt like making bare my very soul before Jesus. I reminded Him that hundreds of thousands had heard Him speak to their hearts and they had given seeds of their faith to bring the construction to where it was, some at a great personal sacrifice. I told Him that it would take much more money to finish the complex and to do the harder work of finishing and equipping the buildings.

He had told me He would speak to my Partners and that He would build it through them. And now I couldn't understand why so many had almost stopped helping me. Why weren't more of God's children hearing Him tell them to be a Partner with me in this project?

Jesus said, "I have spoken to both old and new Partners. I desire them to obey so I can *bless* them and make them a *blessing*. They must get into faith and obey Me. As your Partners obey Me, I will send My angels to stop the devil from stealing their money. And I will do a great spiritual, physical, and financial work in their lives."

By this time I was crying so hard I could barely talk. I cried, "Jesus, You are my Savior; You are my Source. What do You want me to do?"

"Tell the people! Tell your Partners. Make My words known to them. Tell them you want to be the best Partner they ever had, that you are the other part of the partnership.

"Tell them they are not alone with their problems and needs, but that I have anointed you to be My servant and their best Partner."

Suddenly a new flood of tears flowed down my cheeks. My whole being was trembling under the power of the God of Abraham, Isaac, and Jacob. Jesus, in the form I had seen Him, was no longer there. But I could feel His Spirit whipping through me like

a wind,

a fire,

a glory,

a great faith,

a deep obedience.

As I raised my head and looked, the building structure still towered before my eyes. It was a giant empty shell inside, waiting to be finished and equipped. But inside me there was a light turned on to hold back the night that was now closing the day. It seemed I could see clear across the earth and beyond space into Heaven itself. As I looked invisibly into Heaven, I saw a great calm that was opposite to the rushing and roaring I had been feeling in our world.

Then I saw men, women, and children by the untold numbers appear before my vision as if they were cheering me on, and as if they were waiting for the doors of the City of Faith to open to them. They looked like they wanted to touch the glory of God. I saw them not in flesh, but they were real nevertheless.

My mind went to the Bible. I recently had been restudying Malachi 3:10 where God said, "Bring ye all the tithes...and prove Me...saith the Lord of hosts, if I will not open you the windows of heaven, and pour you out a blessing, that there shall not be room enough to receive it." And it came to me that the only thing that cannot be contained is a flood.

It seemed God was saying, "I will give My people not a trickle, not a stream, not a river, but a flood of My blessings and they will be *continuous and endless*. And this is why they never will be able to contain them all." It was an awe-inspiring moment of visitation. I knew those were His words, not mine.

The Criticism Gets Worse

I started my car and slowly drove across the ORU campus up to the house. Evelyn was not there and I waited, because I had to tell somebody.

Soon she came. Richard and Lindsay were right behind her. They looked at me and said, "What has happened to you?"

I said, "Sit down and I will tell you."

And I told them.

As soon as we could, we made a television program and wrote to my Partners about what had happened. When the critics heard the story, they thought the ridicule of my seeing Jesus half again as high as the City of Faith would be the end of my efforts. They reported that Oral Roberts had seen a nine hundred-foot Jesus. But when my letter about this visitation reached my Partners, they understood *in their spirits*. Natural things are natural, but spiritual things are spiritual, and that in God they really belong together. The response of the Partners was overwhelming.

The first month after I had made my plea by letter and on television, we received a million letters. Many of them had a special seed of faith in them and said things such as, "We read the news reports and didn't know what was going on except what they said. Now we know in our hearts this is God moving in behalf of medicine and prayer being joined together."

Immediately I gave the order to start the construction again. Thousands of doubters drove by over the next weeks to see what they thought had been stopped forever. I think they had previously looked at it as more my project than God's. When it is God's, it is different!

In retrospect, when I saw Jesus half again as tall as the unfinished building and received new strength for my faith, I felt I had failed to point out one very important truth. The Bible says that when Jesus returns to fight the Battle of Armageddon with His bridal saints, He will fill the whole sky and space of this planet. "Behold, He cometh with clouds; and every eye shall see Him, and they also which pierced Him: and all kindreds of the earth shall wail because of Him" (Rev. 1:7).

I wish I had brought that out. I know the media would have reported it—not a nine hundred-foot Jesus, but One who fills the whole sky—a billion times the size I saw Him!

IMPORTANT POINTS

1. When God reveals a truth to you, believe it and have faith, no matter how the opposition tries to discredit you.

2. Obey God no matter the cost.

3. When things look the darkest, Jesus will give you a revelation, a word, the invisible, that will help you to keep going.

4. Stay in God's Word when the controversy is the hottest. The safest place is in Him.

15

How I Faced the Controversy of the $8 Million and the Dog-Track Man

What I share with you in this chapter is one of the most heartrending experiences in my life and ministry. I was in the midst of a controversy that almost took my life.

The experience also brought the most misunderstanding from the most people, in high places and low, that came about in that period of 12 months.

As we were building the City of Faith, we were anticipating that the students in the Oral Roberts University Medical School could fulfill their internship there.

I had hired a top local orthopedic surgeon, recently filled with the Holy Spirit, to be the dean of the medical school. He and I sent out the call for a top medical faculty who were either Spirit-filled and understood the purpose of the school or who were open to the idea. A few had come directly to ORU from the mission field. They became role models and a real help.

I had to go to the highest leaders in the American Medical Association to receive approval for our medical school. The chief leader was a born-again believer and believed somewhat in spiritual healing.

When we met to evaluate our purpose for building a medical school, he and I had left the AMA committee and gone into a room by ourselves. I took my Bible, and he his, and I poured out Scriptures supporting world missions headed by medical teams.

I reminded him there were approximately 530,000 doctors in the United States but only about 400 *medical missionaries* in the whole mission field.

As a Baptist layman, whose denomination, along with the Assemblies of God, had the largest numbers of regular missionaries in the nations, he actually gasped at that fact. It hit him hard, as it had me.

"That is why God has commissioned me to build a medical school at ORU," I told him.

"All right," he said. "I'm on your side, and I'll go to bat for the medical school if your main aim is to graduate doctors whose ultimate purpose is to head up missionary medical teams."

I said, "Doctor, that includes Native Americans in North America and isolated areas in the U.S. where there's a scarcity of doctors. We also want to use medicine to open nations now closed to missionaries."

I told him I had ministered in 70 nations and had met only one missionary medical team. I saw where they, with the missionary and his team, had opened up a whole tribe of thousands in Africa to the gospel.

I said, "Since God called me to take His healing power to my generation, I can't fully obey Him without a medical school."

God gave me favor with him, and the charter was granted in 1976. The school was opened at the end of 1978 with eager young medical students who had responded to my call to become trained medical people but also to become part of medical teams, particularly in different nations. I had met with the leaders of some of these nations, and they had said they would take the *missionaries* if I would give them *doctors.*

By November 1981 we had successfully opened the City of Faith Medical and Research Center on campus. ORU already had a top-rated science faculty. We had our third medical team and I was moving along with great expectation in my heart, regardless of the fact that the medical school had the heaviest expense of any of the other graduate schools of Oral Roberts University.

I spent as much time as possible with the medical faculty and with the medical students. I really believed my message from the Lord about raising up medical missionaries was getting through.

I learned later, after our first graduating class went for their internships in the City of Faith and other medical centers, that I *had not* been understood.

ORU had missionary teams ready to go anywhere on earth, all except the medical people. Our nursing school stood by with their missionary nurses to accompany the doctors, but it wasn't happening.

Most of the faculty were in agreement with me, and we kept trying. One day while I was with the faculty, lamenting my pain, I was told what was probably the real reason of our difficulty. They guessed that the students were not making plans to go on the missions field because the cost of a medical education was so expensive. Since these students were not from wealthy families, most would graduate owing $75,000 to $100,000. After internship they felt they had to practice medicine in the States for several years to pay off their debts.

Again I explained to them that I teach my Partners Seed-Faith, the practice that had brought ORU, the medical school, and the City of Faith this far. I operate solely by faith. I believed that if everybody in the ministry and university would operate by faith with me, including the medical students, we could get this job done. If I could start at ground zero on the medical school (and the City of Faith) by faith only, why couldn't they?

My faith stand came back in my face—not from all the medical faculty, but from most. One doctor shed new light on the issue. "We are medical scientists. We've never had to live by faith in the gospel sense as you do. We're just not there yet."

I went out of there blaming myself. I have a habit of following my mother's advice when God speaks to me—"Oral, always obey God."

I had done that time and again. I now learned there was nothing *instant* about medicine. I had not looked into that part of it, nor had I been sensitive to Dean Winslow when he told me that training doctors and sending them on God's mission teams would not be like preparing ministers and other workers. I simply did not hear him. I fault myself for that; it was my mistake.

I probably thought that since I obeyed whatever God said to me, at any cost, every other believer working with me would do the same. What a hard lesson I was forced to learn.

What Happened When God Stepped In

In my distress over the medical missionary scene, I went up in the Prayer Tower, visited with the prayer partners, asked them to pray for me, and closed myself in my personal prayer room.

I was never alone, but I felt like I was. My pain was warping my judgment. I was permitting my problem to overwhelm me. I was full of questions to God. At first I got off on the wrong foot by asking God, *Why?*

I have heard that a loser says, "Why has this happened to me? What have I done to deserve it?" but the winner looks over all the bad things and says, *"What can I do about this?"*

The second day I was in the Prayer Tower I got over my *why, Lord?* and began to get in the Spirit and back in my faith. "What can I do about this?" I asked God. I suppose I had been expecting a quick easy answer.

In that clear, familiar voice I had heard many times before, the Lord said, "Son, I told you to send missionary medical and healing teams to the nations of the earth, which is one of My only ways in opening some nations to the gospel. That is why I instructed you to build the medical school. But you are falling short. I am giving you the rest of this year to turn it around. If you have not started sending the teams out during this time, then your next move will be standing in front of Me telling Me why you have not sent your doctors and others in teams to these nations to heal the sick and save souls."

I felt my stomach start to turn over, and I shook like I had a chill. I was cut so deeply at first I didn't know what was going on.

I told God the problem. I told Him about the debts of the students. "Lord," I said, "I'm doing everything I know to do to believe for enough money to keep the ministry going. Besides, I don't know how much extra money it will take to give scholarships to the medical students so their debts are clear."

God surprised me: "It will take $8 million. I want you to lift the level of your faith to raise it. Even now I am placing a burning desire in your Partners, and in new friends, to help you carry out My plan—even to redirecting some of their missionary giving to this ministry for this project."

As I sought to absorb His words, He said, "Also, I want you to open your Bible and study My Reward System. Write and tell your Partners about My Reward System. Tell them their salvation is by grace, a gift of My mercy. But tell them they will be rewarded by their 'works,' not only when they come up before Me, but *while they are on earth.* Tell them My Reward System is not only a 30-, 60-, or 100-fold return for the seed they plant [He referred me to Mark 4:20], but a *seven-times restoration* of what satan has stolen from them." (See Proverbs 6:31.)

I did exactly as God said in the next few weeks. It went right over people's heads, including my Partners. Now I sure enough didn't know what to do. Yet the words of God continued ringing inside me. I knew He meant business. He would do what He said.

I shared my concerns with the ORU students, who rose en masse to pray for me. During that time I remembered that God had opened my eyes to something. Dr. Luke, a Christian doctor who was Greek, traveled with the apostle Paul. They became a medical/ministry/evangelistic team through whom God did a great work in launching His Church. Later the doctor wrote the Gospel of Luke and the Book of Acts. Paul wrote over half the books of the New Testament. I could see what an all-important assignment God had given me in sending out these special teams.

Toward the end of December, God visited me again. "I told you to raise the $8 million to carry on My medical missionary work. You have from January 1 to March 31 to get it done. If you do not do it, your work on earth will be finished, and I will call you home. You will be standing before Me telling Me why you did not do it."

On January 4, 1987, on our national television program, I announced the $8 million deficit. I told them if I did not carry out God's word to me, my ministry was finished, and God was going to call me home.

It seemed everybody was listening.

I believe the devil was listening too. He, as "prince of the power[s] of the air" (Eph. 2:2), went to work in the most vicious and untruthful way against my life, ministry, and God's higher purpose by blatantly misstating what I said God told me.

The media sent their helicopters flying over the Prayer Tower where they knew I was in prayer and where we were making Richard's daily live TELEVISION program. Many charismatic ministers flew in each week to stand with me in prayer and give their support. They knew I would never falsely report words from God.

The news media jumped on what I had said and misquoted me with headlines like:

ROBERTS SAYS GOD

WILL KILL HIM UNLESS

HE RAISES $8 MILLION.

When the media and hundreds of the highest-placed church leaders jumped on the news media bandwagon, they, in effect, proclaimed that Oral Roberts was a false prophet, was not fit to preach the gospel, and would be good riddance from the world.

The names of these church leaders in denominations, divinity schools, and political situations read like *Who's Who*. Thousands upon thousands of pastors took up the cry and echoed their leaders.

I stood as firmly as I have ever done in this ministry.

> No matter what anybody said or did,
> I knew God had spoken to me, and I
> was dedicated to living out His words.

God said, "I'm going to call you home." The media said, "Oral Roberts says God is going to kill him." Quite a difference in the two statements, isn't there?

The very false way they put it only strengthened my resolve to obey God. At no time in all my years in the healing ministry had I felt satan loose so many of his forces against me, nor had so many human leaders and opinion makers made me the topic of their conversations—and mostly in a mocking way.

While I was in the Prayer Tower, Richard appeared on many national talk shows, such as "Larry King Live" and "Good Morning America," at their request, to explain what God actually said, but it could not stop the tide of criticism from rushing in.

In my spirit, I reached the place where I felt the old faithfuls of God's people—the remnant—were praying for me. I mean, I could feel it! It was like meat and drink to me, for I fasted often during those three months.

The Dog-Track Man

As the time God had set was coming to a close, each day I was able to supernaturally know the amount of donations that came in before anyone told me. When our chief financial officer came over to the Prayer Tower or phoned to give me the amount that had arrived, I would stop him and say, "Let me tell *you* the amount."

He was dumbfounded that the Holy Spirit revealed to me the amount. I explained to him that the word of knowledge works today the same way it did in the day of the first Christians, and that we must never forget God is concerned with every detail going on in His gospel today.

As we approached the absolute deadline of whether God would complete what He planned for the City of Faith and the medical school, a most unusual thing happened to a man in Florida.

One day Evelyn and I were on Richard's daily television program, and Evelyn corrected me on an error I made in giving the difference between the total donations we had received and the amount we needed.

The ORU students always love it when Evelyn corrects me in public. She loves me, she knows I desire to do the right thing, and as my devoted wife, she has the right to speak up when I need correction.

Right on the air, Evelyn said, "Wait a minute, Oral. You're wrong."

"Darling, how am I wrong?"

"You're wrong on how much of the $8 million we lack."

"Well, I've had it right every day. How am I missing it today?"

"I don't know how you're missing it, honey," she said, "but we lack only $1.3 million."

A man in Florida, who owned dog-racing tracks, was watching the show. Turning to an associate, he expressed that we must be honest people. Even if I am Oral Roberts, my wife had the nerve to correct me...and on live television.

He was so impressed he got up and phoned us that he was sending the entire $1.3 million we still needed. The next day he flew to Tulsa with the check. I asked him if the Lord had told him to do this.

"I don't know," he said, "but I know it wasn't the devil."

Everybody in my special room up in the Prayer Tower whooped and yelled and praised God.

"You're a dog man?" I asked.

"Well, I own dog-racing tracks."

"Are you a saved man?"

"I don't know."

I took him by the hand and asked him to repeat after me the sinner's prayer. Tears came in his eyes as he prayed with me. His countenance changed, and we all felt the presence of God filling the room. He and I hugged each other. I thought, *They're shouting in Heaven right now.*

The next thing that happened, the media and some leaders in religious circles jumped on me for taking money from a dog-track man. They didn't realize that in the Bible, God used all kinds of people, including sinners and spiritual outcasts, to do His work. This was true before Jesus came, during His earthly ministry, and later after the Church was launched on the Day of Pentecost. There was the most violent misunderstanding, unbelief, and persecution, including martyrdom of some of God's choicest leaders and others.

In my view, very few people and not nearly enough church members, even preachers, understand this.

To many people the Bible seems to be a book of tales, with some wisdom in it, such as the Ten Commandments, Jesus' Sermon on the Mount, and some of Paul's statements in the Epistles.

Many real scenes in the Bible about God giving the "word of the Lord" to His prophets, His apostles, and later His disciples in the Christian Church, and each with an obligation and a consequence, are not understood by the average believer. They are scoffed at by the world system, which is influenced by powerful news media.

Yet we who have a direct, unmistakable calling from God know that God never plays around by anything He says, commands, and which depends on us.

If we could see the events in the Bible and in our generation and personal lives, I believe we would stop in our tracks, catch our breath, and look at whether we are obeying Him at any cost.

I quoted to my critics what God said. "The silver is Mine, and the gold is Mine, saith the Lord of hosts" (Hag. 2:8).

I said, "All money belongs to God. There is nothing wrong with money; something is wrong only with some people who have it. As for this man, we did our best to lead him to Christ. He felt Christ had come into his heart as we prayed with him up in the Prayer Tower, and he believed he was to give that $1.3 million to the Lord's work."

When that response failed to satisfy the worst critics, I asked different pastors: "Would you have turned the money down?"

Every one of them said no.

The strangest thing of all is that when Evelyn and I went to the man's home later to thank him and his wife personally, he said he had received more than four thousand requests for money since he had given us the $1.3 million. "I read every one of them," he said, "from churches and individuals and different types of organizations."

"Did you send them any money?"

"Not a one!"

The one-time command from God to raise a certain amount of money to complete His mission, the one-time major gift in addition to the thousands of smaller ones, and the one-time focus of the attention of the whole world meant to me: *God intends to merge His healing streams.*

God did not want to call me home. Above all, He wanted what we had built to go on. We felt we had built it under nearly as much opposition as Nehemiah felt when God told him to rebuild the broken-down walls of Jerusalem (see Neh. 2:5).

While his enemies laughed at him, mocked him, then turned to destroy him, Nehemiah, with a trowel in one hand and a sword in the other, alongside his men, restored the walls of God's holy city.

God has not stopped having those who hear and obey Him do mighty exploits in His name.

Soon after we had raised all the money, while Evelyn was attending a women's leadership conference in Washington, D.C., two ladies said to her, "Are you Mrs. Oral Roberts?"

She said, "Yes, I am."

They said, "Then explain to us why God was going to kill Brother Roberts if he didn't raise $8 million."

She said, "But that's not what God said. God said for him to raise $8 million to keep the medical school going, to raise up medical missionaries. He was to announce it on television so the Partners of our ministry would participate. God told him, 'If you don't raise the $8 million, then your work will be over and I will call you home.' The Lord didn't say He was going to kill him. That was the media's term. My husband obeyed God. The money came in, and my husband is still alive and in the ministry."

The women were astonished. They had believed what the media said, but now their eyes were opened.

Millions felt the same way. They were reading the lies of the devil instead of what God said, which is backed up by the Bible.

Some 15 years have passed. Our medical missionary teams are working in many nations. Some have *built hospitals.*

In Ghana I broke ground for Manna Medical Center on the land a chief had given Dr. Seth Ablorh, a 1985 ORU medical graduate, for the hospital. It is flourishing, and prayer and medicine are fully joined. Government leaders told me they are proud of Dr. Ablorh and this new kind of medical facility. And Ghana is totally open to our teams.

In Benin City, Nigeria, my son, Richard, dedicated a new medical center with the country's leaders present. It was established by Dr. Mark Babo, a 1983 graduate of the ORU Medical School.

In 1988, I was with our medical missionary doctors with Jim Zirkle in Guatemala. I prayed while he worked medically with long lines of some of the sickest people I had ever seen. Jim Zirkle and the workers from his ministry headquarters had made our ORU-trained doctor their point man. Their outreach was working exactly as God told me it would.

The last time I was in Africa doing a crusade, I was flattered to be received by the leaders, our American ambassador, and for once graciously reported by the media. It was almost a new experience.

Approximately 300,000 jammed and overflowed the stadium. I preached and ministered God's healing power. It was comforting to have Dr. Seth Ablorh and other medical persons at my side. At the close, a striking, tall young ORU medical graduate sought me out. Learning I was to be there and fearing it was the last time he might see me, he had traveled the day before and all night to reach me.

I remembered his name but had lost news of him. He said, "I head up a medical missions station with another ORU graduate who is a preacher. We and our team have a clinic and a regular route we travel a hundred miles in each direction to do what you told us our ultimate mission was to be."

I said, "Well, how is it with you now?"

He said, "Never been happier in my life. It's not easy but it pays off for God and the people. That's my real pay."

I have learned that time is such an important factor. God says He looks on "a thousand years as one day" (2 Pet. 3:8). Time is on His side, and on ours who obey.

IMPORTANT POINTS

1. God has a reward system for His people who obey.

2. Dedicate yourself to living out the words God speaks to you, no matter what.

3. Let criticism only strengthen your resolve to obey God.

4 God decides the avenues to take and the people He will use to help you accomplish His calling on your life.

5. Time is an important factor in accomplishing God's vision.

Part Three

IDEAS
CONCEPTS
INSIGHTS

16

How One New Idea Multiplied My Success in the Ministry

Everything operates on an idea. Without fresh, new ideas, your life and work fall flat.

In 1946, I accepted a pastorate in Enid, Oklahoma, so I could continue my education at the university. Shortly thereafter, I received one of the biggest shocks of my life.

Usually when someone accepted a pastorate, they were furnished with a parsonage or another place to live. But this church furnished us no place to live. Without money of my own to rent or buy, we were stranded after I had preached on the first Sunday morning. We literally had no place to go!

Finally, after we stood around for a while, a member of the church invited us to stay a few days with them in their little two-bedroom house. Well, that stretched into several weeks. No matter how I asked the church board to help us, nothing happened.

Then we found out this kind man who was letting us stay in his home was being transferred through his job to another city. My family was about to end up in the street!

This family had gone to extraordinary lengths to accommodate us in a house with their three children, and Evelyn and me with our first two. Added to the cramped conditions, there were two women in one kitchen!

After learning of the family's being transferred, Evelyn said to me, "Oral, if you don't get a place to live for these children and me, I'm going with them to my mother's" (who had a two-story house).

I said, "Evelyn, you wouldn't!"

She said, "You just watch me!"

Evelyn was not able to go to the prayer meeting that Wednesday evening, so I went alone to preach. Believe me, I was anointed! I preached like a man from another world! I shared our dilemma in my message. As I was closing, the Lord spoke in my spirit, "Start the down payment for a parsonage by giving your week's salary." I thought my stomach was going to fall out.

My salary was $55 a week. Only by living with this generous family could we buy our share of the groceries, dress decently for my church work, and pay my school tuition, which included a discount they allowed to all ministerial students. My old car would scarcely run, so I had to ride the bus, which cost twenty cents each way each school day.

Out of sheer obedience, I took out my $55 check for the previous week and laid it on the altar. "Folks, I'm led of the Lord to give my week's salary toward the *down payment* on a parsonage, not only for me but for the pastors who will follow." I had seen the invisible, and now I was ready to do the impossible.

Then I said, "Who else would like to help?" To my surprise, folks jumped up all over the sanctuary and laid money on the altar. We counted it and found it was enough for a down payment.

When I arrived back at our friends' house, Evelyn asked me how the service went. "Oh, just fine," I said. "I got the down payment on a parsonage. You won't have to take the children back to your mother's."

"How much did you give?" she asked.

"I gave the best I could."

"How much?"

When I told her, she said, "Oral! How do you expect me to have money to buy groceries for these children next Saturday?"

"But, darling," I said, "the Lord impressed me to give our week's salary. That's what caused them to give and enabled me to have the down payment."

It was winter, and I slept in a cold bed that night. I thought to myself, *I could drive a truck between her and me.* My next thought was, *What am I going to do?*

At 4 a.m. I was awakened by a loud knock on the front door. When I opened it, Art Newfield, a member of the church, was standing there. He said, "Pastor Oral, please forgive me for waking you at this hour of the night. Would you please let me in?"

"I'm in trouble," he told me. "I've been playing the stock market without knowing how, and I'm about to lose everything, including my farm. I was there when you gave your week's salary to help get the down payment on a parsonage. I didn't give anything. I went home but couldn't sleep. A half hour ago I got up, went out into the yard, and dug this up." Reaching into his pocket, he handed me four $100 bills.

Now I had never had a $100 bill in my life.

He said, "That is not just money I'm giving you. It is seed. As you know, I'm a wheat farmer, and I know I have to plant seed in order to have a wheat harvest. I'm sowing this seed to you as a man of God for the Lord to get me out of this trouble I'm in, so I can get back to farming, something I know how to do."

Evelyn was looking around the corner of the bedroom door. I went over and just shook those four $100 bills in her face. As we rejoiced, it dawned on me that in about seven hours the Lord had multiplied back what I now understood for the first time was a seed. My $55 salary I had given was a seed out of my need, a seed of my faith.

Evelyn and I didn't go back to bed but sat up talking about seed. My mind began to race over the many different places in the Bible where God had given His people seedtime and harvest (see Gen. 8:22); sowing and reaping (see Gal. 6:7); giving and receiving (see Phil. 4:15). Jesus described His core teaching in these words:

> Whereunto shall we liken the kingdom of God? or with what comparison shall we compare it? It is like a grain of mustard seed, which, when it is sown in the earth, is less than all the seeds that be in the earth: but when it is sown, it groweth up, and becometh greater than all herbs, and shooteth out great branches; so that the fowls of the air may lodge under the shadow of it (Mark 4:30-32).

> ...If ye have faith as a grain of mustard seed, ye shall say unto this mountain [of need], Remove hence to yonder place; and it shall remove; and nothing shall be impossible unto you (Matthew 17:20).

I remembered how I had been raised mostly on a farm until I was 14 years old. I knew how important seed planting was. To produce a crop, my dad, my brother Vaden, and I first plowed up the ground, laid it open in deep rows, planted our seed for cotton, corn, and other things, then covered the seed with a harrow.

As the seed grew and covered the ground, we hoed and cut the weeds away, cultivating the seed so it could fully grow and multiply. When that was done, we "laid the crop by," and began looking forward to harvesttime, which was always rejoicing time. We raised cotton and other produce to sell, pay off our bills, buy new clothes, and carefully put enough seed in the barn to plant another crop the following spring.

I had never connected natural sowing with reaping in a spiritual sense, linking it, as the Bible says, with what the apostle Paul called giving and receiving. I had missed the *key issue*.

This was such a fresh new idea that I could hardly contain myself. Enthusiasm for giving burst forth within me. I had never been more excited since my conversion and healing and call to preach.

I had been raised in a church where the pastors taught giving, but they said nothing about receiving. In fact, they taught the opposite: Giving was a debt we owed to God, but expecting something back was selfish. We should consider our giving only as a sacrifice we had made.

A new slogan came up inside me.

**Giving is not a debt you owe
but a seed you sow.**

For the first time I really understood. "Jesus paid it all" on the cross. If we had all the money in the world, we couldn't pay our debt to Him. This eventually led to my discovery, *God is a good God*, and many other such new revelations that have since become the trademarks of my ministry. Also, these revelations have been incorporated into much of the theology of the Church.

This idea of giving and receiving brought about a desperately needed change, a fresh breeze of enthusiasm for God, a contagious joy that we could give out of our need and expect the Lord of the harvest to multiply our seed sown and meet the needs for which we had sown.

That is exactly what Art Newfield did in that little house when he handed me seven times what I had given that night. In the weeks to come, Art went back to what he knew worked: sowing and reaping. His farm was saved, and he became one of the most prosperous farmers I ever knew.

Evelyn and I changed the way we tithed. As I have said, we were taught to give but not to ask God for anything back or to expect anything. We were to give ten percent and live on the ninety percent. Not only had we stumbled along with this kind of lifestyle, but so had every church I had pastored. Consciously or unconsciously, the church people did not want their pastor to prosper. Neither did the community expect the ministers in their midst to prosper.

They expected us to live just below the average income of the members of the church, being humble and proving we were not preaching the gospel for money.

Little did they realize that if the pastor did not prosper, he could not inspire them to prosper. If they did not prosper, the gospel could not be spread.

Jesus' words in Matthew 24:14, "And this gospel of the kingdom shall be preached in all the world for a witness unto all nations; and then shall the end come," could never be fulfilled without the resources to do so. Sowing and reaping from the spiritual area had never reached the people's understanding.

It was this attitude that later showed me why there were so many Christians who had an inferiority complex and who worked and lived with low expectations, and also why the outreach of the Church to the community and the nations of the earth was not more extensive.

A fresh new idea was that all these problems could be changed by simply obeying the Scriptures. We can follow the examples of those in Bible days, like the believers in the church at Philippi. The apostle Paul taught them giving *and* receiving. He wrote that in return for obeying in their giving, "My God shall supply all [ALL] your need according to His riches in glory by Christ Jesus" (Phil. 4:19).

Before this I had been afraid to reveal I had a new suit, or to try to believe for a new car, or to live in a nice home with my family. I tried to be content with as little as possible. I knew something was wrong with this kind of thinking and believing. Until God opened my eyes with this fresh new idea from Art Newfield, I was losing the joy of my salvation and of my ministry.

I wonder about you. Have you subscribed to the general teaching that you are to give sacrificially only and not expect miracle returns?

I want to tell you that the eternal laws of God in the Bible say:

receiving does follow giving

reaping does follow sowing

harvesttime does follow seedtime

and you are to expect miracle returns!

Including financial!

God has a better way for you to carry on your personal life and work and to be a leader in your community who is respected and who gets results.

IMPORTANT POINTS

1. Everything operates on an idea. You must have fresh new ideas from God to succeed.

2. Giving is not a debt you owe but a seed you sow.

3. As you allow God to prosper you through giving and receiving, you can inspire others to prosper and help spread the gospel.

4. If God's people don't prosper, we cannot take the gospel to the world as a witness to all nations for the end to come and to bring Christ back (see Mt. 24:14). This is an awesome challenge and responsibility. But I believe God's Seed-Faith people can do it! Don't you?

17

HOW I LEARNED TO LOOK TO GOD AS MY SOURCE

I n the darkest period of my need, at that precise time, God intervened purposefully in my life. Yes, the Art Newfield experience had followed the special giving of my week's salary.

The first thing I did was to start looking for the supply I had received to *continue* rather than being a *one-time event*. I saw that the bottom line—the heart of the matter—in the Word of God was sowing your seed to produce a harvest, then expecting to receive that harvest so that all your needs could be met. That is when the term, *the Miracle of Seed-Faith*, came into my spirit with its three divine keys for God to meet all of our needs.

The miracle of Seed-Faith was like a neon light shining in the darkness, giving me a clear opening of a whole new future when I would no longer be a loser but a winner. I was seeing the invisible; therefore, doing the impossible was just around the corner.

The three keys of Seed-Faith came into my mind and spirit with a powerful force and gave me new insight into the hidden riches of God, which I had not known existed the first 12 years of my ministry.

The three keys of the miracle of Seed-Faith are:

1. Look to God as your source.
2. Plant your seed.
3. Expect a Miracle Harvest.

I seized on the revelation knowledge of the three keys, particularly the first key: God is my Source of total supply, not man. That is the key on which I want to share revelation in this chapter.

I saw the error I had committed for so long. This was also the error of my preacher-father, other believers, and really the Church in general. I had never noticed in my Bible and my other study materials that from the beginning God had made Himself the source of all life and the all-continuous supply of life.

He is the Creator, the Father of us all—and the One who so loved us (even the whole world, including the family He had created and lost) that "He gave His *only* begotten Son, that whosoever *believeth* in Him would not perish, but have everlasting life" (Jn. 3:16).

Through studying Abraham's life and Paul's writings, I came to understand God is the Source of our total supply.

In the account of Abram, whose name was later changed to Abraham (father of many nations), he and his 318 trained servants had just returned from pursuing the four armies who had taken the surrounding cities captive, including his nephew Lot. At that time God sent Melchizedek, the priest of Salem (later Jerusalem), to bless Abram; that is, to pronounce not just *a* blessing but *the* blessing of the most high God.

Read it with me:

And he blessed him, and said, Blessed be Abram of the most high God, possessor of heaven and earth: and blessed be the most high God, which hath delivered thine enemies into thy hand. And he [Abram] *gave him tithes of all* (Genesis 14:19-20).

Four major things stood out to me. Melchizedek said:

- Blessed be Abram of the Most High God,

- Possessor of Heaven and earth,

- and Deliverer from all thine enemies,

- and Abram gave him tithes of all.

The light shone through—Abram was unlike those of that era who worshiped idols of their own making and placed them on the highest hills. He saw God who is most high—highest of all. He saw that God owned both Heaven and earth equally. Satan did not own one inch of ground or drop of water—all was the property of the Most High God.

As Abram had faced these four conquering enemy armies and with "a few defeated the many," he saw God as *the One* who delivered him from *all* of his enemies.

As a result of seeing God in this dimension, he reached into his possessions and gave Melchizedek "the tithes of all." Abram gave the priest of God the top ten percent of all he possessed from his victory.

As I meditated on Paul's statements in Galatians 3, that we today who are of faith are Abraham's children, I saw that our faith comes from him. And we who are "in Christ" are Abraham's seed.

In other words, faith runs in a direct line to us from 35 hundred years ago in Abraham's time when he first discovered God as His Source. Today we take the counterpart of the old covenant and bring it into the new covenant of our Savior, Jesus Christ of Nazareth. So the same four major things that Abraham discovered about God now stand out to us.

- God owns the earth and its fullness (see Ps. 24:1) and all the silver and gold in the earth (see Hag. 2:8) and all things come from Him (see Jn. 1:3).

- The Most High God is shown through His Son Jesus, whose name is above every name (see Phil. 2:9).

- God, who delivered Abraham from all his enemies, is in our New Testament as the One "[who] shall supply all your need according to His riches in glory by Christ Jesus" (see Phil. 4:19).

- We sow all our tithe as seeds of our faith to God as the Source of our total supply.

I Was Missing Whom to Trust in My Life and Ministry

Heretofore, I had been almost totally looking to man and to things for my supply. Man or things are not the Most High God; nor is their name above every name; nor do they possess Heaven and earth; nor have they the resources and the power to be our Source. I was looking in the wrong place.

Let me tell you a true story that illustrates this. My Uncle Willis Roberts had a big orchard on his farm. His best money-making crop was the famous Elberta peaches. He sold hundreds of bushels every year to people who came from far and near to buy.

My brother Vaden and I helped him pick the peaches, pack them, and carry them to the cars of the buyers. One year we found him very discouraged. "Uncle Willis, what's the matter?" we asked.

"Boys, during the last two or three years my peach trees have been producing less and less. Well, I've just had the country agricultural agent out to find the reason why. After examining each tree and the soil around it, he told me what the trouble is."

"What's that, Uncle Willis?" we asked.

"He told me I had made a fatal mistake. I had paid attention to the *fruit* but very little to my *trees*."

"What does that mean?" we inquired.

"Well, it means I haven't been plowing around the trees, stirring up the ground so the air and rain can get in. As a result, my trees have grown stunted. My peaches have been growing fewer and smaller each season."

With a sad look, he said, "Boys, there won't be many peaches this year."

"What'll you do?"

"I'm going to do what the agriculture agent said. Plow up my trees and plant new ones in their place. Then I'm going to take care of those trees, and I'll be sure to have a good crop every year."

Learning about God being our Source, I remembered that scene. I had to face the truth. God was trying to get me to understand that I had been paying attention to my blessings (the fruit) but not focusing on the Source—God as the giver of my blessings.

My faith was misdirected. I was looking to those I ministered to instead of God, in whose name I was ministering. The returns were small and getting smaller.

I preached the gospel; gave my full time, talents, and knowledge of God's inspired Word; and prayed for the people both publicly and privately. I was looking to them to supply my financial needs. *I was looking to those who were not God, who alone is our Source.* Poverty and want continued to embarrass, hinder, and hold me back, lowering my self-esteem, robbing me of my faith to raise the hopes and expectations of the people.

I was guilty!

I had to admit to myself that I, Oral Roberts, one called of God to minister His gospel, had been weighed in the scales of trusting man rather than God as the Source for supplying my needs.

Further, I had allowed this omission and failure to understand the *key issue* of the Bible to penetrate and embitter me until I wanted to quit. Have you been there?

In Galatians 6:7-9, I read:

Be not deceived; God is not mocked: for whatsoever a man soweth, that shall he also reap. For he that soweth to his flesh shall of the flesh reap corruption; but he that soweth to the Spirit shall of the Spirit reap life everlasting. And let us not be weary in well doing: for in due season we shall reap, if we faint not.

I learned that if I (1) looked to the God of the harvest as my Source, (2) sowed my seed, and (3) expected my miracle supply to be sent to me from both expected and unexpected sources, and if I would not become weary (discouraged) in my well doing, *in due season I would reap a full supply for all of my needs to be met.*

It was mind-boggling then, and still is now, 54 years later. I finally learned to use the key, God is my Source, at all times and in all situations.

I saw it as clearly as I did the noonday sun. I was ministering God's Word. I was speaking in His Name, and now I must look to Him as my Source, the Author of all my blessings. *I was not to be thinking of who would support my ministry or how much that support was to be.* I was to hold Him in the center of my trust.

My expectation must be to receive exactly what I was scripturally guaranteed I would receive. Therefore, from that hour, it would be like God and I were working arm-in-arm. His miracle touch would be on everyone to whom I was ministering and upon assignments I was led to perform

I remember the weight that lifted off my shoulders, how light I felt inside. I could obliterate from my mind what *man* could do for me and concentrate on what *God* could do for me. He would do what no one or anything could do to supply all of my need.

Psalm 23:1 filled my mind: "The Lord is my shepherd; I shall *not want!*"

IMPORTANT POINTS

1. Always look to God as your Source—not to people or things.

2. God is the Most High God, possessor of Heaven and earth, and delivers you from all your enemies.

3. In giving God your tithes, sow them as seed to Him your Source and expect Him to multiply your seed sown—and be in a conscious attitude to receive.

4. Realize you're working with God and He's working with you through the miracle of Seed-Faith.

18

How I Discovered That Everything Begins With a Seed

A major change came into my understanding concerning the basis of *God's giving* and therefore what must be the basis of *our giving*.

Everything begins with a seed. Giving is based on a seed. Our faith works as a seed.

God linked seedtime and harvest, sowing and reaping, giving and receiving into the same thing. They are one and the same throughout the Bible. In God's dealings with His people on why they are to give, He tells us to associate our giving each time with receiving. Receiving follows our giving.

A harvest cannot happen without first planting the seeds. You cannot fulfill God's call on your life without first planting your seeds. In other words, you cannot do the impossible (receive the miracle) without first seeing the invisible (planting the seed).

As I indicated, I was once muddled in my understanding of this eternal principle of the Word of God.

We preachers often fail to teach John 3:16, the core verse in the Bible, from the perspective of *how* God gave and *why* He gave—and how those aspects apply not only to our believing for eternal life, but also to the meeting of our needs.

For example, in John 3:16, I saw that GOD *aimed* the giving of His Son, who is the seed of seeds. The Word calls Jesus the seed of the woman (see Gen. 3:15), the seed of Abraham (see Gen. 17:9; Gal. 3:16), the seed of David (see 2 Sam. 22:51), and the seed that God sowed for a purpose: *that He might receive His lost family back!*

I looked at John 3:16 as if I'd never seen it before:

For God so loved the world, that He gave His only begotten Son, that whosoever believeth in Him should not perish, but have everlasting life.

- God not only loved, He *so* loved.

- He loved so much that He *gave*. All giving in the God sense is based on our love.

- What did He give? His worst? NO! He gave His *best*, His only begotten Son. He had only one to give. Out of love He gave Him to die for our sins and to rise again for our salvation.

- He gave for a *desired* result. His giving was His seedtime, and His seedtime was aimed at His harvesttime. His multiplied return was receiving back hundreds of millions of His lost family.

- He gave out of His *need*, His want. "Oh, but we're not to expect anything back," I'd heard all the time. Well, why not apply that same logic to God here?

Did God have a need, a want? How could God have need and want? Isn't He God?

When He decided to have a family whom He could love and who would love Him in sweet fellowship, He created Adam and Eve to "be fruitful, and multiply."

But Adam and Eve allowed themselves to be seduced by satan (lucifer, the fallen archangel) in the Garden of Eden. In breaking God's law, they fell from their divine estate and lost everything. So did God—He lost His family. His *need* was to get His family back. There was one way: plant His best seed, His only begotten Son, on the cross. And He sowed that seed.

- He sowed with *expectation* of a miracle harvest. It began to happen and is still happening. It includes you and me as His sons and daughters.

- He *received*! And He is still receiving as souls are brought into His Kingdom, helping to restore His family.

Now *that* is the background I use for tithes and offerings, because a person can apply that to his own need and want.

When we "so love" as God did,

sow our best seed as He did and does,

sow our seed for a desired result,

aim that seed as He aimed His Son,

expect to receive our harvest of multiplied return, then...

you can't talk us out of giving...of sowing our best seed!

God led me to Luke 6:38, which reads:

Give, and it shall be given unto you; good measure, pressed down, and shaken together, and running over, shall men give into your bosom. For

183

*with the same measure that ye mete withal it shall
be measured to you again.*

We are to do the first thing: *give*. Once we take the first
step back to God's way of sowing first, giving first, then God
follows by giving us a multiplied return—our miracle harvest—
seven different ways.

Following our step of giving first, Jesus said these seven
things would happen:

- It (what you give) shall be given to you again

- Good measure

- Pressed down

- Shaken together

- Running over

- That men shall give to your bosom (into your life);

- With what measure you mete (give), it shall be measured to you *again*.

These are truths that we preachers should be sharing
with people over and over. The Holy Spirit will use these and
other Scriptures to instruct them, to open their hearts, to
reveal to them that giving initiates receiving.

Once we give by *aiming* our seed for a desired result
(harvest), we are to expect...expect...expect. When it comes,
as it surely will, we will *recognize* it and reach out and receive
it, instead of letting it pass us by, then saying, "Well, I gave,
but God gave me no harvest."

Once I began learning this directly from God's Word, my
life changed. I began to feel honored to explain this eternal
principle of giving and receiving, for I knew it would meet the
needs of believers—and our receiving would put us in position

to really and joyously see our own needs met as we could support God's work.

My spirit had been greatly distressed at the average reaction of people toward giving to God's work. Their feeling often was that many of us preachers are in it for the money, that the Church is always after them to give money.

Unlike most preachers, I have been subjected to the news media *big* time. In every interview by newspaper and television, everything finally comes around to money. If they come to the services, they look for the offering to be taken. If they bring their television cameras into the services, they focus on the offering plates or cups being passed. They seek to make that the number one reason we are having services of the gospel.

Behind some of the secular media are secular people, who resent any preacher or church who prospers. They want him or her to remain poor, and the church to be the same.

As ministers have been breaking out of the poverty syndrome, these same people think of offerings primarily as a device to get people's money. They seem to want to separate money from life...from being the medium of exchange for believers as much as it is for the world system.

"Reverend Roberts, how much money do you make?" is their number one question to me. They do not seek any information on how many souls I win, how many are healed, how my ministry builds up the Church, or how we have built a major university based on God's authority and the Holy Spirit while being academically strong.

"You preachers are taking money from the poor and getting rich," many of them constantly say. They promote this idea in their media.

Both secular and religious people who object to Christian prosperity can see in the Bible that Abraham (the father of all who have faith) and others were rich. But dealing with God's leaders today is a different story.

When they read about the men of the Bible prospering, it is acceptable, but it is not acceptable today. Especially is that true of people who believe in signs and wonders as Jesus taught us to believe.

Another paradox to me is how we treat money. Money can be used to support God's leaders as they to carry the gospel into all the world and bring the power of God to supply the needs of the people.

Yet in the typical Sunday morning service, when the tithes and offerings are to be received, there has been very little teaching from (all) of God's Word on giving and receiving. Pastors seem to have been intimidated and the spread of the gospel suffers. It is a shame unto God, who owns it all!

So unbelief and disillusionment began to form in our hearts. What is not said is the worst of all, and I have been guilty of this, to my regret.

Our giving of money is not *just money*, but is a seed we sow into the good soil of the gospel. God will multiply it back to us in the form of supply for all our need! The miracle of Seed-Faith will give us peace of mind, a good attitude about our giving, and a continually expectant heart.

How I Learned in My Losses and Defeats to Sow a Seed for an Equivalent Benefit

Over the many years of my ministry I have discovered there is no way I can avoid having some losses and suffering some defeats.

Too many times I have let these bother me and sometimes really get me down. I sought God to help through His Word, through prayer in the Spirit, and through squaring my shoulders and bearing up in order not to be hindered in my obedience to God.

When you are in the limelight as long as I have been, your losses and defeats are easier seen by others, increasing the pressure on your spirit. Of course, whether you are exposed to large segments of the public or not, any loss or defeat hurts your heart.

I had to find a way to overcome problems that are impossible to avoid, due either to satan's planning or sometimes by my own stupidity or failure to pay attention or to keep my mind on God.

The Lord showed me a way to overcome these hindrances, these things I felt were so hurtful, not only to me personally, but to other people to whom I was a symbol of a higher calling.

He showed me where Seed-Faith is most helpful. He told me to sow a seed for an equivalent (equal) benefit in every loss or defeat and that this could wipe out the setback and produce a miracle harvest He has especially designed for this type of attack against me.

As I was searching my Bible for examples of where His servants did this, and trying to understand how to do it myself, I remembered an incident from my farm days.

A hailstorm battered our house, driving us to the storm cellar. The next morning we found the storm had wiped out the seed we had just planted: cotton, corn, and other staples, including our garden fruits and vegetables for the table, plus canning for the winter months. The damage was so great our hope of having a crop to harvest was completely gone.

My dad, my brother Vaden, and I walked over our fields where we had planted our seed. Now everything had been beaten into the ground.

We had spent all our money. It was a terrible time for us. Our loss was devastating.

My mother, a plucky never-say-die type, went into action. "Ellis," she said, "you've got to replant."

Papa said, "Claud, it's too late to put more seed in the ground. Besides, we don't have the money to buy the extra seed."

Mama knew papa "farmed" us boys out a few days at a time to help other farmers, for which we were paid. "Boys, how much money do you have left?" she asked.

We counted it and laid it on the table. My dad always carried a $20 bill in his wallet. Mama said, "Lay it on the table, Ellis." And he did.

She pulled down a small jar from the kitchen cabinet. In it was her savings, which she had put away every chance she had. On the table it went.

All of the money came to approximately $100. Papa said, "That won't buy enough to plant 160 acres."

Mama said, "Take it, Ellis. Go to Mr. Jeter's feed store in town and spend it on seed."

He said, "It's no use; it's not enough!"

Mama prevailed and off we went. Mr. Jeter knew my dad and offered his sympathy. He told us that the hailstorm had knocked out most of the farmers in the county.

Papa told him he wanted to buy seed to replant. Mr. Jeter told him not to waste his money. It was too late to plant.

Papa laid down his money. Mr. Jeter realized it was far short of buying all the seed needed to replant. I guess something touched his heart. Instead of telling Papa it was not enough, he told us to drive our wagon around to the back. He said, "Your money will buy all the seed you need."

With our wagon loaded, off we went to plow up the soil again and sow our seed. I learned later from the Lord that we were *sowing out of loss for an equivalent benefit.*

As we were planting, Dr. Burns, the country doctor who had delivered me, happened to drive by in his buggy. Seeing us and knowing of our loss he stopped, got out, crawled through the fence, and came to where we were.

"Ellis, you're planting again?"

"Yes, it's our only hope."

"Well, let me tell you something. Delivering hundreds of babies in this part of the country, I've had some medical losses and failures. Many times when it seemed all hope of saving the mother or the baby was gone, I redoubled my efforts and spent extra hours, refusing to give up. Many men and women now grown owe their lives to my dogged determination, and of their fathers not giving up either. You're doing the right thing. I believe you'll grow another crop and you'll forget you lost the first one."

I remember his words to this day.

Somehow, some way, after we got the seed sown, it took hold and soon came up, and weeks later we had a bumper crop!

Because he was the only farmer who had replanted and new cotton was scarce, Papa got almost double price for our bales of cotton. We filled our barn with corn, harvested our wheat, and there was great rejoicing at the Roberts' house.

How many times have I felt a loss was the end? Felt like quitting? I learned to immediately plant a new seed of my faith when it seemed it was all over. God's eternal principle of sowing for an equivalent benefit took hold of my loss and wiped it out!

The Book of Acts describes how the apostle Paul's ministry in Philippi was broken up when he and his associate Silas were thrown into jail. Defeat seemed total. Paul and Silas sowed a new seed. At midnight they sang and prayed to God, who sent an earthquake that shook the jail, and their bands fell off.

The jailer thought they had escaped, a situation that under Roman law meant he would be executed. He decided to take his own life. Paul cried, "Do yourself no harm. We are all here." (See Acts 16:19-28.)

After the jailer saw they were still there, he took Paul and Silas to his home. Paul explained what God had done and led the jailer and all his family in accepting Jesus as Savior. Out of this equivalent benefit the Philippian church was established. Then when Paul was run out of town by the city officials, he simply took his ministry to the next city of Thessalonica where he established another church.

I assure you that failure, loss, and defeat need not stop your calling or even seriously hinder it. You have seed to sow. Go ahead and sow it by faith. Look to God to grow your seed sown, trust Him as your Source, expect a miracle harvest, and you will see what God will do.

One of my worst seeming defeats came in a foreign country where we had taken our 10,000-seat tent and equipment. Crowds overflowed the big tent from the opening night. Thousands stood around outside hoping to get a glimpse of the miracles.

Then a dock strike hit the city. The Communist dock-workers heard of the crusade. Having nothing to do, they came in their drunken state to break up the meetings.

There was no law at that time in that nation for protection of such religious meetings. Those dockworkers rushed down the aisles and began spitting on me and hitting me until I could not preach or pray for the sick. They also stopped people from coming forward at my invitation to the unsaved.

The police did nothing. That night on the way out of the tent to the car, several of the mob sought to kill me. The pastors took me another way, and I escaped with my life.

The next day the news media came out with headlines, "Mob to Burn Roberts' Tent Tonight." The international insurance company wired that they were canceling their coverage if we stayed. The U.S. ambassador told the sponsoring pastors he had no authority to protect us.

Without my knowing it, during the night my men had taken the tent down, loaded our semi-trailers, and put them on the ship home. Evelyn and I were awakened at daybreak and rushed to the airport onto a U.S.-bound plane before the mob knew it.

Talk about defeat...loss...and the worst media coverage imaginable. Tears flowed down my cheeks. I felt that satan had at last stopped my ministry.

Plant a seed out of your loss for an equivalent benefit, kept resounding in my spirit. As soon as we reached Tulsa, Evelyn and I took our biggest offering to the church we attended, telling the Lord we were looking to Him as our Source of total supply, and were sowing this seed to overcome this defeat.

We still hurt. The critics were having a field day. Two of the most prominent Christian magazines wrote terrible articles, blaming us and not the mob.

Mama Roberts called me to her house and sat me down. "You're doing God's work, son," she said. "You keep looking to Jesus. This will soon be behind you, and your ministry will get bigger and bigger for God."

What a mother I had!

Two things happened that year of 1956. The defeat had occurred in January, but that year turned out to be the year of our largest attendance at crusades in America. Nearly two million people came to the crusades that year. It was the first year when the big tent was filled, and often overflowed, in every service in every city where we ministered. The unsaved came to Christ by the tens of thousands. Miracles of healing greater than we had seen before began happening and in larger numbers.

We found out that in the country where we suffered such loss, new churches sprang up out of the several thousand souls we had won before the defeat.

Prior to our crusade, healing was scarcely heard of there. Today healing has spread across the nation. Big crusades similar to mine are going on all the time.

My son Richard went on a preaching/healing tour in that nation. He was welcomed everywhere. The media couldn't say enough positive things about his ministry. The television stations carried him *live* several times.

Most importantly, the laws have been changed by the government to protect religious meetings.

One year after my crusade, my warm friend Billy Graham held a huge crusade in that country. Learning of what happened to me, he sent me the following telegram:

"Dear Oral, I know that you had a rather difficult time here, yet for your encouragement I have met many people that were blessed through your God-anointed ministry."

Since that time the equivalent benefit has produced Oral Roberts University, and our ministry rolls on for Jesus. My advice in bad situations is to plant a very special seed for an equivalent benefit and watch it happen!

Remember, if you stop and plant your seed to God in any type of loss, that loss will not be fatal to you. Don't give up; plant your seed!

IMPORTANT POINTS

1. You must plant a seed before you can reap a har-
    vest in your life and do the impossible.

2. Just as God aimed the seed of His Son to bring the
    harvest of humanity back to Him, so you must aim
    your seed toward your need.

3. In every loss or defeat, sow a seed for an equiva-
    lent benefit.

19

How God Taught Me to Expect a Miracle

During the height of my healing ministry, we had record-breaking crowds and multiplied thousands being saved and healed, but there was also a wall of opposition at times. In Miami, Florida, in one of my crusades, I received a message about an organized effort to physically stop me from preaching and praying for the sick.

This type of thing had happened before, and I had pretty well adjusted to it. I trusted God to protect His servant and repel the efforts of the enemy to stop His visitation of healing power.

The people opposing me were a notorious group of atheists who were known for their vicious, unrelenting attacks on all Christianity, especially against preaching confirmed by signs and wonders. They threatened not only to break up the crusade but also to place a citizen's arrest on me and have me thrown into jail to bring embarrassment to the ministry and my name.

The Miami crusade was so successful it occurred to me that the devil was not going to ignore it. There was such a visitation of the mighty power of God that satan had to bring out his biggest gun and most evil plan to destroy what God was doing among the people.

The group was led by the nationally known leader of the atheistic movement. There was something so sinister about this plan that when I was warned of it, I felt a cold fear clutch my heart. My spirit knew this was a different tactic.

I usually took a short nap around 3:00 p.m., so I would be fresh to preach and pray for the multitudes who came to be saved or healed or both. This time I fell across the bed, deeply disturbed and unable to sleep. I tried to pray, but it seemed a force came against any words from my heart and lips to God. Then suddenly God spoke to me audibly.

"My son, expect a miracle!"

Astonished, I said, "Lord, would You say that again?"

He said in a clear voice, "Expect a miracle!"

I had never heard that term before or thought of expecting a miracle. As I pondered these words, He spoke again,

"Expect a new miracle every day."

"From this time on tell the people to expect
a miracle and to expect a new miracle
every day."

Immediately my fear left and I fell asleep. I awakened with a powerful anointing upon me. My staff, along with the sponsoring pastors, had alerted the police, who were dispersed throughout the crowd as I entered the service. The news media, having received hints from the leader of the atheists of what they were going to do, were there with their cameramen and reporters.

Walking to the stage, I had never felt so fearless, ready for whatever happened. There was a tension throughout the place. You could feel it. As I preached, not a thing happened. It was like a covey of angels had visited and cleared the enemy out. There was a spiritual breakthrough of such proportions that the place erupted. Over one thousand people in that service came forward to accept Christ as their personal Savior, and the healings were beyond the usual.

I had told the audience about God's visitation to me in my room. I repeated His words to expect a miracle, and to expect a new miracle every day. The people were electrified, and as the visitation of God's saving and healing power swept over us all, I felt I had a fresh new word from the Lord. I began sharing it everywhere I went and on our television program.

"Expect a Miracle" struck a responsive nerve across America. A new sense of expectation for miracles seemed to break out everywhere.

I began to tell the people, "Miracles are coming toward you or past you every day. Expect a miracle so when the Lord sends it you will recognize it and reach forth and receive it. The miracle will come, but if you are not expecting it, it will pass you by. You will wonder why God is not visiting you in your time of need and trouble."

I wrote all this down in a little book, *Expect a Miracle*. Over a million people ordered it. It became a classic.

I began to hear those words repeated in religious programs on TELEVISION and radio. Wherever I went people would smile and say back to me, "Expect a miracle." It was like a greeting.

Norman Vincent Peale, minister of the Marble Collegiate Church in New York City and founder/publisher of *Guideposts*, came out with articles in *Guideposts* headed by the words, "'Expect a miracle' is the most powerful statement to change your life." And so it went, even to other nations.

My whole attitude changed. Bursting with a new enthusiasm, I saw my ministry results increase dramatically. The following year we recorded a million souls being saved in an 11-month period, the first time we were able to record such an amazing number of souls saved.

Jesus said we must know the time of our visitation (see Lk. 19:44). Peter wrote, "Glorify God in the day of visitation" (1 Pet. 2:12).

You can be absolutely positive that God will visit you. Miracles will flow toward you. As you get into the attitude of expecting miracles, more and more will come toward you.

The *key issue* is recognizing a miracle when it comes.

If you are not continually expecting God's miracles, a new one every day, it does not mean they will not come. They will. However, as you expect them, you are in a position to be open to *receive* them by *recognizing* the signs that your miracle is coming your way. If you miss seeing the invisible, you will not be able to do the impossible.

I once read through the entire Bible looking for examples of God's visiting His people with miracles. I was impressed by how often this happened to individuals and groups. I also saw how many times they were not looking for the miracles, failed to recognize them, and the miracles passed them by. I saw the times when there was weeping and wailing because they thought God had either forgotten or forsaken them.

It seems to me that God's people all too often miss expecting a miracle from the living God. I know I have blundered in failing to do what the Lord told me: to expect a miracle and to expect a new miracle every day.

I think satan is especially riled up over this word from God, and of this being God's time of visitation to each of us in the most personal way. But I am committed to being more observant of miracles He is sending toward me.

I am very encouraged to see a new surge of interest in this truth. People are coming right out in the open with their expectation of a miracle. This is so important because *a miracle settles the issue.*

On one of my world trips, I was conducting a crusade in Taiwan (formerly Formosa) when a miracle settled the issue in a most tense situation.

At first my reception had been great. General Chiang Kai-shek and his lovely wife had received us at the palace and we had prayed together. Taiwan, a heavily armed little nation because of its nearness to China, had taken a great interest in the crusade. Several of the colonels and generals were Christians. They had invited me to speak to all of their top leaders, and I had done so.

At least half of the audience at the crusade were soldiers with their leaders. They mainly stood along the walls of the auditorium, as all seats were filled with civilians.

In my call to the healing ministry, God had directed me to first preach; second, have invitations to the unsaved; and last, pray for those who needed healing, a number that was always large.

In this crusade, on the third night I sensed a terribly wrong hostile feeling coming at me from the crowd. Those whom I was touching and praying for were not getting healed. It was a new experience for me and very disturbing.

At the end of the service, the chairman of the sponsoring pastors told me, "The Chinese don't like to be touched. They are not used to it. That's the reason miracles are not happening."

"What must I do," I asked, "since that's my guidance from the Lord Himself?"

He then advised me to explain to the people that when I lay hands on them I mean no offense, but I am giving an expression of my respect and love for them. The highest honor I can give them is to minister as the Bible says, by the laying on of hands, to help them release their faith for God to heal them.

The next night I gladly did that, but I did not feel much change in the attitude of the audience.

During the healing time a woman with a large goiter protruding from her neck stood before me. The goiter could be easily seen by everyone. All eyes were focused on her and me as I explained to her that my touching the goiter with compassion and faith was because I respected her. Would she please receive my touch in that spirit? My interpreter explained this to her, and she nodded yes.

Before us all, as I touched that awful thing on her neck that was choking her, and prayed, it instantly and completely vanished. The flesh on her neck was suddenly loose. She put her hand on it and began to cry and rejoice and praise the Lord.

I heard a loud noise. Hundreds of soldiers rushed the platform, demanding to see where the goiter had gone. The interpreter carefully explained that God had used my hands, my faith, and the woman's faith to perform a miracle.

When they heard that, they crowded around me and asked me to lay hands on them! The end result was the conversion of scores of these young army men on the spot.

The Lord spoke in my spirit: *A miracle settles the issue!*

Thereafter news of the meetings spread through the island. We left a deposit that I believe is still there. I have received many letters from people high and low who remember the statement I made as the slogan for the rest of the crusade: "A Miracle Settles the Issue."

However, the Lord has continually reminded me in His Word and directly in my spirit that miracle-receiving must be handled with care. The miracles may seem to come at random, but that is not true. Somebody or groups of somebodies have been believing and expecting miracles. A seed has to be planted first.

God's eyes move over the earth. He knows what is going on in all human hearts. He always has a remnant of faithful ones who diligently stay the course with Him and His works on earth. I believe He depends on all of us to be part of that remnant.

I am one who gradually learned to remember every day and in every situation not to despair or give up, but to expect a miracle and watch for it. I learned to look for the signs, and to be instantly ready to recognize it and reach out and receive it.

I call this to your attention, man and woman of God, whose call is on your life. You can be a leader in this, and doubtless you are.

My prayer is that God will speak to more and more of His preachers and other leaders about the meaning of miracles. He has always done His work by miracles, and the Bible is filled with references to how miracles settled issues and brought victory to His cause.

There is so much more than what has been revealed to me, far more than I have experienced. I believe countless numbers of miracles are on their way toward us—and I believe toward all people everywhere. I feel driven to share how God has dealt with me about miracles and what He has done in and through my one life by miracles of His love and power.

IMPORTANT POINTS

1. The *key issue* is to recognize when a miracle is coming toward you.

2. When you plant your seed and expect a miracle, you are in a position to be open to receive it.

3. A miracle will settle the issue in your life.

20

WHY I MAKE NO DECISION OR ATTEMPT ANYTHING FOR GOD WITHOUT FIRST PRAYING IN THE SPIRIT AND PLANTING A SEED OF FAITH

For the first 12 years of my ministry, I did too many things randomly or without the proper preparation of myself to make right decisions or attempt something that required divine direction and the power of God.

As a result, I was wobbly spiritually. I had no pattern for my life. I could make no definite decisions nor attempt great things with any degree of confidence that God was in them.

I was full of ideas, some quite creative, but I could not bring order and direction to them, or bring them to fruition with a knowing they would work.

Yes, I made some good decisions, attempted some good things. However, I was often torn in attempting these, ending up double minded. As the apostle Paul said, I was making an uncertain sound. (See First Corinthians 13:1.)

Oral Roberts and Billy Graham, 1967
"Sow a seed, pray in the Spirit, and watch
your impossible dreams come true."

Something had to give, to change in me. This crisis brought me to the climactic choice of my life and ministry: to continue in this unsettled condition or to find the way I knew existed in God. *But how would I do it?*

By the end of those first 12 years, I had determined I would study my Bible with a total desire to find out how men of God such as the apostle Paul made their God-ordered decisions and attempted the projects the Spirit led them to do. I wanted to see how they saw the invisible and therefore did the impossible.

In particular, I studied the nine gifts of the Spirit that are listed in First Corinthians 12:4-11:

> *Now there are diversities of gifts, but the same Spirit. And there are differences of administrations, but the same Lord. And there are diversities of operations, but it is the same God which worketh all in all. But the manifestation of the Spirit is given to every man to profit withal. For to one is given by the Spirit the word of wisdom; to another the word of knowledge by the same Spirit; to another faith by the same Spirit; to another the gifts of healing by the same Spirit; to another the working of miracles; to another prophecy; to another discerning of spirits; to another divers kinds of tongues; to another the interpretation of tongues: but all these worketh that one and the self-same Spirit, dividing to every man severally as He will.*

I was particularly taken by the gifts of the word of knowledge and the word of wisdom, as well as discerning of spirits. This came to be called revelation knowledge by many people.

The gifts of tongues and of interpretation of tongues fascinated me but I could not grasp them in a practical way.

I was baptized with the Holy Spirit and had spoken in tongues occasionally, usually at a point of deep distress or deep joy. I could not speak in tongues (in the Spirit) *at will.* I had to wait until they spontaneously flowed up from my belly area (my inner man). I had no idea I could interpret back to my mind (my understanding) God's response to my praying in the Spirit.

I really did not know tongues is either praying in the Spirit or singing in the Spirit. I had not been taught much on this. In a pivotal moment I learned how to pray in tongues at will and also interpret back to myself God's response. It happened in 1963 when I did not know how to do what God had spoken to me to do.

The Lord had spoken audibly into my spirit in May 1935, while my brother Elmer was driving me to the service where I was to receive prayer for my healing from tuberculosis and a stammering tongue. He said, "Son, I am going to heal you, and you are to take My healing power to your generation. You are to build Me a university based on My authority and on the Holy Spirit."

This was clear and definite, and I understood the *first* part of what God had spoken to me.

The second part about someday building Him a university was not so clear, but I knew I had heard Him speak it to me. At age 17, I was too young to grasp its significance, but the fact was inescapable to my spirit.

I had no idea how to build a university, especially to build *God* a university. Although I eventually attended two universities, I knew nothing about building or operating one.

The main thing in my favor was that I had made a life's determination to obey God. My mother had counseled me all my life, "Son, always obey God, and stay little in your own eyes."

Although I had stumbled around in my ministry, sometimes missing the track, I was committed to obeying God in every way I understood. After 28 years of ministry, 21 of them in the healing ministry—I knew God's time had come for His university to be built.

> God had driven this into my spirit—*success without a successor is failure.*

Soon my healing ministry would peak. If I had not paid attention to raising up successors, despite all the good I had done in reaching the masses of my generation with God's saving and healing power, it would end mostly with me. God wanted His work to go on, to improve over my efforts, and to continue to increase and fill the earth.

Everything was moving just fine until it was time to build, to create the university. God had told me, "You are to build the university out of the same ingredient I used when I made the world—nothing!" That had shocked me to the roots of my soul. I had seen the invisible (the vision), and now it was time to do the impossible—*but how?*

Each day I drove out to the university site in Tulsa, Oklahoma, and walked over the bare grounds. One day as I walked over the whole area, I prayed for God to show me how to undertake this massive and complicated project.

I had no money, no buildings, no faculty, no students, no know-how, and few who believed I could accomplish this.

I had never felt lonelier in my life. My mind was as blank as a sheet of paper. I had only the *knowing* inside that I had to obey God by starting with nothing.

I burst into tears and fell to my knees in desperation. Suddenly a language from the Holy Spirit flowed up over my tongue. I had no idea what I was saying, although I knew that when you pray in tongues you are speaking to God.

First Corinthians 14:2 says, "For he that speaketh in an unknown tongue speaketh not unto men, but unto God: for no man understandeth him; howbeit in the spirit he speaketh mysteries." I knew I was speaking mysteries. I was invading that celestial realm where all true knowledge and wisdom reside.

It lasted only a minute or two. I rose to my feet, not knowing what to do next. Suddenly words in my own language began to pour forth from my mouth, revealing knowledge I had been lacking.

Instantly I cried, "Lord, let me do this again." God let me do it again, and again.

When it all ceased, the clouds had lifted, the dawn had broken, and light from above flooded my mind. Suddenly I saw how to build God a university based on His authority and on the Holy Spirit, and have a strong academic foundation. *I saw it*—the buildings rising, the faculty coming, the curriculum appearing, students pouring in from across America and the nations of the earth. It was a crystal-clear vision. I had seen the invisible.

I drove home and shared all this with Evelyn. She was heart and soul with me but did not understand what God had spoken inside me about building Him a university.

The next morning she passed the bathroom where I was shaving and heard me praying in tongues. Her first thought was: *O God, Oral has been so balanced in his healing ministry. Please don't let him go off the deep end now.*

Although Evelyn had spoken in tongues like I had at emotional times in life, she did not understand interpreting back to yourself what God was saying. Later that week God touched her to ask me to explain about tongues and interpretation as I was manifesting them in this new endeavor. I explained to the best of my knowledge at the time and had her read First Corinthians 14 with me. Then she asked God to let her have the same experience. And He did!

From that time, we prayed in tongues together, and she too learned she could interpret back to her mind God's response.

In First Corinthians 14:13-15 Paul says we can use our will to pray in tongues and to interpret back to our understanding (mind). We receive God's revelation knowledge.

Let me say an important word about revelation knowledge, the revealing of God's Word by the Holy Spirit in ways you cannot find for yourself by studying the Bible. Some say all of God's words to us are written in the Word of God. There is nothing more God has to say. But since the Holy Spirit was poured out on the Day of Pentecost, He has been speaking and is still speaking by revelation knowledge from the Bible to believers, and particularly to those who preach and teach the gospel.

The Holy Spirit knows how to personalize what God is saying to you in His Word. To me this has been very important.

Revelation knowledge given to you must line up with the Word of God and be confirmed by it. It is not a jumping off in every direction or wild imagination. That can lead to forming a cult or joining one. If revelation knowledge is not confirmed by the written Word of God, forget it.

When God calls you to do something, you can give yourself wholly to Him and expect Him to equip you. He may not confirm this up front, but as you take each step, more of His plan and His will will be *revealed* to you.

As I said earlier, I had no idea how to build a university. Revelation knowledge played a major part in helping me to invade an area unknown to me but known precisely by the Holy Spirit.

So, I saw how to carry out my assignment, but *doing* it was another crossroads, one I had never crossed before. What to do next?

The first thing I do before making decisions and attempting things for God is to pray "in the Spirit" and with "my understanding." The second thing I do is to *plant a seed of my faith*.

As clearly as I had heard God speak before, He told me to plant my seed of faith so I could receive all the things I had seen in the vision.

Evelyn and I had accumulated a small estate. We sold our investments and gave the proceeds as the first money to start building the university. We understood this was not just money, but seed. It was seedtime and harvesttime, sowing and reaping time, giving *and* receiving time.

Seed-Faith had become our way of life in obeying God and in attempting things for Him. When my seed went into His hands this time, a load heavier than any I had ever felt lifted off me.

I had received revelation knowledge solidly based on the Word of God. I was first to pray in tongues with the interpretation,

Without God's revelation knowledge and planting seeds, I could never have fulfilled the big plans God called me to do—and neither will you.

then sow a seed of my faith, before making any major decision or attempting to do anything God had placed in my spirit.

Those two actions of my faith may seem to make little difference, but that little difference has made all the difference for me in being successful for God!

If you come to Tulsa and drive to 7777 South Lewis Avenue, you will see over 400 acres with 22 major buildings, thousands of students, and a major university fully accredited in higher education. And you will see my son, Richard, the second president and CEO, operating Oral Roberts University better than I did as founder and president for the first thirty years.

ORU is a center of the charismatic movement, educating the whole man with undergraduate, masters', and doctors' degrees, all undergirded by God's authority and the Holy Spirit. It is as much a miracle to me today as when I first saw it in my spirit and began building it, as God said, out of nothing.

A sign on my desk in my office says "Make No Little Plans Here." Without God's revelation knowledge and planting my seeds, I could never have fulfilled the big plans God called me to do. I say to you: make NO little plans where you are.

IMPORTANT POINTS

1. I want to emphasize that I make no decisions or attempt anything for God without first doing two things:

    Praying in tongues and receiving the interpretation as the apostle Paul did in First Corinthians 14:13-15.

    Sowing my seed of faith, giving God something to work with to multiply into a miracle harvest to bring to pass His plan and purpose.

2. When God calls you to do something, He will equip you. As you take each step, He will reveal more of His plan.

3. To help you, God will give you revelation knowledge, the revealing of His Word by the Holy Spirit in ways you cannot find for yourself as you study the Bible.

21

FIVE SECRETS I LEARNED FROM MY MOTHER THAT HAVE INCREASED MY MINISTRY

My mother, Claudius Priscilla Roberts, stood only five feet tall, a little over a foot shorter than I, and ten inches shorter than my father.

She did not have a loud-speaking voice as my father did.

She did not seek the limelight but was content with her quiet callings to say a right word in season (see 2 Tim. 4:2; Is. 50:4) and to pray for the sick—not so much in public services but what we would call "on the side."

She had the unusual ability to get to the *key issue*, the bottom line, of situations and circumstances. She quickly knew if it was satan at work or the Lord Jesus present to answer prayer. My father knew her strengths and depended on her to discern what was going on, either good or bad.

What I learned from both of them was priceless.

These are the five secrets I learned from my mother, whom I called Mama.

#1. I Must Give My Personal Testimony

She believed that if I did not tell what God had done and was doing in my personal life, my preaching would sound hollow and be without the power of God to relate to people and their needs.

I grew up at a time when preachers believed the best preaching was to interpret Scripture by using other Scriptures. In other words, once they established their text and subject, they would refer to other experiences in the Bible that related to what they were preaching.

This approach helped their listeners to know more about the Bible. It certainly had its place, then and now.

All too often they failed to also tell how those Scriptures related to their own lives or to the lives of others to whom they had ministered.

It was just straight Bible preaching without a personal testimony.

Mama loved the Scriptures, and she loved to hear my father (whom I called Papa) preach. But I heard her say in the quiet of our own home, "Ellis, you didn't tell how God and the Scriptures helped you, or your family, or somebody who was healed or saved or delivered after they heard you.

"Think about how little the typical person in your audience knows about the Bible. Some don't possess a Bible. They enjoy hearing you explain these Scriptures and tell how they worked miracles in people's lives thousands of years ago. But what they're hungry for is, 'What does it mean to me? How will it help me out of my troubles? How does it help me now?'"

Papa was not one to share his personal experiences very often in his sermons. He counted on the Word of God he preached to do the work in people's lives. That is not all bad. He established 12 churches in totally new areas. He was anointed to preach and even we children enjoyed hearing him.

Mama was not a preacher, but she was a housewife who had a living, walking, talking relationship with Jesus. She did not know the Bible as Papa did, but she knew the Jesus of the Bible. He was as real to her in her time as He had been to people when He was physically on earth. She was able to listen to Papa's sermon and get the bottom line of the Scriptures he used and bring them right down to her needs and to the needs of others. That is what preaching meant to her.

We children saw a pattern forming. Papa did the preaching and made the invitation to people to be saved or to be baptized with the Holy Spirit. As they came to the altar to pray, he would sit down and give the nod to Mama to take over.

She prayed with those at the altar until they prayed through to salvation or the baptism with the Holy Spirit or for some other need. She loved doing this, feeling it was part of her calling. Papa knew her value in this area and told her so.

Mama spent time with me concerning the value of weaving into my sermons my personal testimony of how God had saved me and healed me from tuberculosis and stuttering.

She would say, "Oral, make your sermons come alive with what Jesus has meant to you personally, what He means to you this very hour. Bring the Bible down to where people live."

Thus, when you hear me preach on any subject, I am likely to bring in some part of my salvation, in-filling with the Holy Spirit, or the miracles of my lungs and tongue being healed. I share not only my experiences, but also God's miraculous intervention in others who received something special from Him through my ministry.

I want Jesus to be alive in me every second and to work through me as He worked His miracle power in Bible days. I want to feel keenly alive in my spirit. I want to feel a constant renewing of my mind by the Holy Spirit. I want to be a "new creature in Christ" at all times and in all situations.

That does not mean I do not spend countless hours studying and meditating on God's Word or comparing Scripture with Scripture. My burning desire is for people who hear me teach and preach God's Word and bring healing, as they did in Jesus' time and the disciples' time, to be able to relate to what I am giving in the most personal way.

A preacher without a testimony is one without a "now" message, and that falls short of meeting people's needs in the NOW of their lives.

#2. Obey God and Stay Little in My Own Eyes

I think Mama had my number. She discerned me, including my weaknesses and disposition in the ways I related my life to the world.

"Son, always obey God," she said to me often. She sensed that any disobedience I had toward God would cause me to fail, to fall. The main thing to her was *obey God*. Her words got deep inside me. To this day, obeying God is the number one thing I am concerned about. My first thought always is: *What does God say? What does the Word say?* Whatever balance I have in my ministry starts with obedience.

The secret of deliverance is in instant obedience.

I have found that to be absolutely true.

"Son, always stay little in your own eyes." Mama sensed in her spirit that when I began to be successful in my calling,

I would be tempted to have the big head, to boast, to claim the credit as though I had done some great thing. She had seen this spirit destroy some other truly called men and women.

Within the deepest part of my being, I know without God I am nothing. Without my salvation and healing and obeying His call, I would, as Mama warned me, develop tuberculosis again, and my tongue would stammer and stutter again. I would die prematurely, as I would have done just hours before Jesus saved and healed me and gave me His healing call.

I am far more afraid of praise than I am of the doubters, the scoffers, the ugly-acting ones toward me. A Baptist pastor friend of mine in Tulsa told me, "Oral, to smell perfume is good, but to drink the bottle is poison." I believe that. I enjoy praise in small amounts, but I refuse to listen to more.

Thank you, my precious mother.

#3. Ask Myself the Right Questions Concerning Opposition to My Life and Ministry

At one point the news media ridiculed my healing ministry, and some of the church leaders came down on me with the force of their office to take away my ordination papers.

I was used to this kind of treatment for doing what Peter, in Acts 10:38, described Jesus as doing: "How God anointed Jesus of Nazareth with the Holy Ghost and with power: who went about doing good, and healing all that were oppressed of the devil; for God was with Him."

He went about doing good!

Yet the opposition never ceased; it culminated in His death on the cross at age 33.

As this kind of treatment continued and never abated, Mama pulled me down to her and said, "Son, when you're opposed, when the enemy says all kinds of things against you, when the devil tries to make you believe they'll destroy you, remember this:

"First, ask yourself, is it true?

"Next, if it is not true, consider the source."

Thankfully, I had a listening heart. I knew she had never led me wrong. I believed in her and the wondrous way she discerned the truth through God.

Hundreds of times, encountering the side of the world and those in the Church who have said and done everything in their power to misrepresent, oppose, and destroy me, I have stopped and asked myself:

"Is what they are saying and doing to discredit my ministry true? If so, how can I change? If not, why would I change?

"Who are these people, these negative forces, these who misunderstand? Where are they coming from? What is their nature? What source do they represent?"

Talk about bringing strength to your inner self—your real self. Those questions have been ministry to me!

Think about it in your own life. *Just who is it, Jesus, coming against me so hard? Why are they coming against me? Is it true what they are saying? Right what they're doing?* These questions will lead you to answer yourself honestly. You will change—if the change does not change God's call on your life. If the opposition is untrue, you will consider the source and get on with your calling. Leave the outcome to Jesus.

#4. Under No Circumstances Was I to Strike Back at My Enemies

Mama kept talking to me about a real devil. The devil is going to be the devil, and if I had a lot of God in me and I was lifting up His name, the devil would cause certain ones to be my enemies, *big time.*

"Oral, it isn't always the person himself, or the group themselves, who will turn against your ministry. It's the devil's business to try to stop anyone who is damaging his kingdom. He will use anyone or any group who will listen to his lies. You may think it is those people, but it's really satan you're fighting against.

"You must learn how to recognize the difference. Instead of striking back at a person or a group, turn your faith against satan and command him to take his hand off God's property—you!

"Above all, *never strike back!* If you strike back, the devil has succeeded in taking your mind off God and your calling. He has confused your mind—until, instead of having a sweet spirit when you minister, you will communicate bitterness to the people.

"Trust God in this. He's stronger than you think. He's more concerned than you are about your withstanding all the attacks, however dishonest they may be. Also, people are harder to fool by your critics than you may think. If they see *results* in your ministry, if they are *getting* help, they're not going to believe all the negative stuff.

"And, son, one other thing. You'll never develop without coming up against hard and difficult things. Remember, Jesus, Peter, Paul, and all of them in Bible times became strong by focusing on God and their calling rather than getting their eyes on those who hated them. Remember what is said about Jesus, 'Looking unto Jesus the author and finisher of our faith; who for the joy that was set before Him endured the cross, despising the shame, and is set down at the right hand of the throne of God' (Heb. 12:2)."

I give thanks to Jesus for giving Mama such wisdom as this. God knows I have committed myself to *not striking back!* Whatever sweetness I have from Jesus in my life and calling, it is due in great part to my *practice* of never striking back. I just trust that if I obey Jesus, stay little in my own eyes, and do my work without expecting a lot of praise, He will take care of me and my ministry.

#5. The Explosiveness of the Anointing

I learned that God anoints not only His preachers and teachers but also each of His people, if they only know to receive and use the anointing for His glory.

Mama was an anointed woman. Not a loud woman. Not a talkative woman. But one who, when she talked, carried an anointing that enabled her to say what she wanted to in very few words.

For example, when my father was in a hard area where there was strong unbelief against his preaching, he would often call on Mama to come to the pulpit and testify. He knew her testimony could change the atmosphere of the service before he stood up to preach.

Mama had the uncanny ability to share no longer than three or four minutes before the audience would open up and respond, even to the point of jumping to their feet to praise God. I saw this happen time after time, even in the last years of her life when she came before the ORU student body and faculty at chapels.

She was a woman of few words, but the anointing she had through her closeness to Jesus caused her words to have a zing, to penetrate one's very soul quickly. In fact, the secrets I have shared with you were given in few words, even fewer than the words I used to describe them.

In my ministry I have tried to make every word count. I have tried not to preach until I knew I had the anointing. When I have succeeded in doing this, God has done great things.

I gratefully carry the memory of my precious mother in my heart.

IMPORTANT POINTS

Five secrets my mother taught me:

1. Give my personal testimony to others.

2. Obey God and stay little in my own eyes.

3. Ask myself the right questions concerning opposition to my life and ministry.

4. Don't strike back at my enemies.

5. God's anointing is explosive.

22

FIVE SECRETS MY FATHER TAUGHT ME THAT ARE STILL GOOD TODAY

I have been a learner, a student of preachers of the gospel. I cannot think of one I did not learn from, even if it was something I should never do. I believe it is very important to see both the strengths and weaknesses of those we hear preach and teach the Word of God.

I've already referred to the poverty syndrome my preacher-father had. It was not his true heart, however. It was there because of the time in which he lived, his denomination's stand on their ministry members not prospering, and the general mood of people against the gospel in areas where Papa ministered.

His family suffered because of this. There were two reasons I left home to make my own way. One was my own burning desire to shake off a religious culture that was not education-minded and held no big dreams for their children. The other was that the world they lived in was too small for me. I rebelled.

I remember as a small boy standing on our back porch, looking over the hills of Oklahoma, and imagining that big world out there—a world that beckoned to me to rebel and break loose someday. At nearly 16 I did just that, saying in my heart, "World, here I come."

I am not saying my father and his denomination were totally wrong. They were good people, honest, hardworking, and sincere.

They were strong on holy living. They sought to build character in all us children. Although their dreams were small, they held the righteousness of God for your life as the highest priority. Looking back I see many good things that helped shape my life and taught me to listen to God's voice. I owe them much.

What I learned from my father in the midst of the world he lived in made a real mark on my ministry of preaching, teaching, and healing. I think you will find these points helpful in a very personal way.

#1. The Priceless Secret of Loving the Bible

Months after I had left my parents and home, I was fighting against the current to reach my goal of being a lawyer and someday reaching the heights politically in my state. Precious memories of Papa's love for the Bible flooded my soul. Unlike my mother, who read everything she could get her hands on—including the Bible—Papa read very little beyond his treasured Bible.

I remember him with his chair leaned against the back of our house, his Bible in his hand and his Cruden's concordance nearby. As a child playing around him, I noticed him reading his Bible. At times his body shook as tears fell from his eyes. Or I heard him give a whoop of praise to God. He had found something in the Bible that often made him leap or shout for joy.

He would stop and hunt through his concordance, looking up corresponding Scriptures, completely absorbed in his search for the core principles of God's Word.

Many times he would call us children to him and read the great Bible stories to us:

the creation of man,

Noah and the flood,

Abraham's daring journey to an unknown land he sought by faith,

Isaac and Esau,

Jacob's ladder,

Joseph sold by his brothers into slavery and his prison experiences for crimes he had not committed,

God bringing him forth to be Pharaoh's right-hand person,

Esther's brave deed in saving the Jews,

Jesus' birth,

Mary's sacrificial faith and obedience as a young girl to bring forth the Christ child...and on and on.

Papa was a gifted storyteller. He made the people in those stories live. He did not just describe them, but through his words he took us where they were, and let us see and hear and feel them and their faith.

I did not know these Bible stories were having a lasting effect on me and that I, too, would become a preacher. I, too, would preach not only major points of the Bible but also would take people to scenes in the Bible that could change their lives. I owe my father the credit for this powerful secret of molding my sermons inside a story.

Many preachers came to my entire crusade just to hear my sermons on "The Fourth Man"; "Samson and Delilah, Battle of Champions"; "You Can't Go Under for Going Over"; "Transferred Power"; "The Master Key to Healing"; and "Demon Possession." They came time after time to hear these same sermons. At the end of this book I have given you my sermon on "The Fourth Man." I encourage you to take from it whatever God reveals to you. It has had and still has more impact on people's lives than any other sermon I have ever preached.

I am told that in Africa today scores of native preachers have my book of sermons with "The Fourth Man" in it. They memorize it and preach it word for word, and they are having the same results in souls won and sick healed as I did.

To this day I remember my father, who had little formal education, preaching the great themes of the Bible—always in story form. I hear myself saying, "Thank you, Papa, for teaching me this most powerful form of bringing the Word of God to life for those who hear me."

#2. The Preacher Must Have Integrity

Papa's word was his bond. People could trust him in whatever he promised to do.

He hated debt, refusing to borrow money except as a last resort. Even then, he could not wait to pay it back, and in most instances paid it back before it was due. He had an impeccable credit rating.

To the extent of his understanding, my father talked the talk and walked the walk to the day he went to Heaven at age 87.

Not having integrity is like not having a name or a country.

I know this: Without integrity I never could have accomplished the things God called me to do.

Through the years, when I learned of a preacher who did not have integrity but would not change, I wiped him or her off my list. One preacher-friend told me, "Oral, I've noticed when you are approached by preachers whom you can't trust, you treat them in a manner that says, 'Get integrity or get lost.'" I had to admit he was right.

As I have studied the lives of people in the Bible whom God used the most, their integrity and obedience stood out above all else. I believe it is the same today.

#3. The Intimate Presence of Jesus Can Be With Me at All Times and in All Places

My parents usually awakened about 4:00 in the morning, and we children would hear them talking to Jesus. That is among my most precious memories. I came to believe that Jesus lived at our house. Believe me, that marked my life. This secret of my father and mother has never left me.

I have proven to myself over and over, whether I am home in America or in any of the seventy nations in which I have witnessed, that I could have Jesus *in* me and *with* me every moment and everywhere. There is never a time I do not know He is in me and with me. It is like Paul said, "Christ liveth in me" (Gal. 2:20).

4. The Secret of the Absolute Reality of Heaven and of Hell

My father knew the Bible teaches there is a hell to shun and a Heaven to gain. More than that, Heaven was always as close to him as his next breath. He talked about the uncertainty of life on earth and the certainty of Heaven when "we die in the Lord."

Reaching out to his three sons and two daughters, he kept before us the importance of knowing Jesus, of serving Him on the earth, and of reigning with Him in Heaven throughout eternity. He told us hell was not made for man but for the

229

devil. If anyone rejects God, he will not be sent to hell by the Lord but will choose to go there as an intruder.

No one can read the Bible with an open mind and fail to see how the Lord has prepared a hell "for the devil and his angels," and that we are intruders if we choose to go there; or that He said, "If I go away, I will prepare a place [Heaven] for you" (see Jn. 14:2).

I did not know how deeply this was getting inside my spirit, my consciousness. At age 17—when I knew I was about to be taken out of this world by the incurable disease in my body—the truth about Heaven and hell came to my mind again and again.

I, in turn, have taught this secret to my children and my children's children, as well as to all who hear me preach. In no way do I flinch from proclaiming the truth of a living Heaven and a living hell. It affects me, and I never forget it.

5. Bless My Children Not Only During My Life, But at My Death Time

This is what Papa did. He knew he was going to Heaven when the revelation came to him at age 87 that he was going to die. On his final day, he sent for his four living children— Elmer, Jewel, Vaden, and me.

We each knew in our hearts that our father was leaving us. We entered the room and stood by his bed, aching inside.

The doctor told us his heart was just giving out. His health had been amazingly good. We had loved his strong, healthy body and the unmistakable look of Jesus' presence shining through his countenance.

Still we were sobered by the reality that our father was at last going to his eternal home about which he had talked and preached.

He took each of us by the hand and blessed us, saying words of love and hope, and spoke of his expectancy to see us in Heaven someday. "God bless you," he whispered, and he was gone. We bent and kissed his cheeks, our tears flowing. We had no doubt that he was absent from the body and present with Jesus (see 2 Cor. 5:8).

Later, whenever all of us were together, we never failed to bring up our father's name, or something about him we remembered. At all times he was with us. We knew the kind of man of God he had been.

I cannot tell you how much my father's blessing us at his death was a reflection of his life and ministry. Already I know I want to put a blessing on my children at my homegoing. It lives in me. And I know my children are expecting it.

As my father continued preaching in his seventies and eighties, so am I—with the deepest appreciation of this gift from the Lord, and for the joy set before me, that when I die I am going to Heaven!

IMPORTANT POINTS

These are the secrets Papa taught me:

1. Loving the Bible is priceless.

2. Preachers especially must have integrity.

3. The intimate presence of Jesus can be with me at all times and in all places.

4. There is an absolute reality of Heaven and hell.

5. Bless my children during my life and at my death time.

23

FIVE SECRETS I LEARNED FROM EVELYN, MY WIFE AND LOVER

I f I had filled this book with only the secrets I have learned from my darling wife, Evelyn, I believe I could have filled every page with very useful material.

The Lord Himself sent her into my life because He knew what my needs would be as a husband, father, and preacher of the gospel. Fortunately, I realized she was the chosen one for me.

I have loved no one so completely as I have loved Evelyn, and I have learned as much from no one. From the time we both were 21 to this hour when we are 84, we have understood this marriage is of the Lord and He is doing a work in us of supreme magnitude.

Let me share with you the secrets I value the most that I have learned from being married to Evelyn. These have helped fulfill me, first as a man, then as a husband and father, and in my calling.

#1. The Secret of Putting Our Family First in Our Lives

Evelyn reminded me that God created the family before the Church. He expects us to lead our family to Jesus—not let them go to the devil and to hell while we are trying to reach the rest of the world.

It takes love, patience, and time to nurture children. They watch every step we take. Many times they take their responsibility in life in the way they see us take ours.

At first our children did not understand why I had to be gone so much in my healing ministry; I was home approximately one week each month. Being so intense in my ministry, I made a lot of mistakes as a father. Had I known then what I know now, I would have done things differently. We have only one opportunity to share quality time with our children while they are growing up.

It is a miracle that as many preacher's children accept the Lord as do, even when their parents are so busy with the gospel.

In our marriage Evelyn had to assume the greater part of the load because I simply was not there. When I was home, I was so hungry to spend time with Evelyn that it seemed I ignored my children. They felt I did not pay much attention to them.

I remember one of the first serious talks Evelyn and I had about this. I called her into the den, closed the door, and said, "Evelyn, there's something wrong with our marriage. When I come home from the crusades, you and the children seem thrilled that I'm home, and for the first day or two it's just like we're in Heaven. Then all of you go your own way and ignore me."

Evelyn said, "Oral, I love you with all my heart. I spend as much time with you as I possibly can. But our children have needs and daily schedules they have to meet. As their mother, I can't ignore them. You don't know what a normal marriage is like since you're seldom home more than a week at a time."

She hugged and kissed me, and let me know how much she loved me (which I knew was true). I said, "Darling, I'll try to remember that."

We finally resolved to spend as much time together as we could. I carved out as much quality time with the children as was humanly possible.

2. The Secret of Controlling My Temper

I have always had a quick temper and reacted to circumstances or people I did not like without even thinking. How many times I wished I could call words back. I was explosive.

Evelyn would say to me, "Oral, keep your voice calm. Don't get upset, and remember what the Bible says, 'A soft answer turneth away wrath'" (Prov. 15:1a).

Oh, that was hard for me. I was so quick. Thank God, as I grew older (particularly at my present age) I have learned to take things a lot easier.

In those early days, I found myself talking to God about my temper and other shortcomings with which I seemed to have been born. I did not like any of those things about myself. Evelyn pointed out that at times I was rude but did not intend to be. I loved her even more when she was honest with me like that. I did not stalk out of the room, get in the car, and drive away sulking and resenting her.

In my heart I was trying to follow the truth, which is:

It is not who is right,

But what is right.

Believe me, I did not find it easy to do that. These sins of my personality seemed to be deep inside me and rose up at every opportunity. Sometimes I would stop and say, "Evelyn, pray with me. I need your faith with mine so I can overcome these enemies to my life, my family, and my ministry."

Those prayers together, often with us hugging each other with tears, began to make a definite difference in me.

Finally, Evelyn was able to say, "Oral, you're getting more mellow. You have a much kinder spirit." I give God the glory for that.

With His help, I learned we can harness anything.

3. The Secret of Using Good Grammar

Having taught English, Evelyn knew and spoke good grammar. I had loved English in school and had learned good grammar, but I had become careless in the way I spoke the English language.

She told me, "Oral, lift the people up with good grammar. Do not pull them down." That really woke me up.

I asked her to correct me on every mistake in grammar she heard me make. I told her I would not resent it. In fact, I ordered a special correspondence course in grammar. She and I began studying it together.

She told me I was splitting infinitives and using double negatives. I used too many colloquial terms, such as "ain't," which was not considered good speech. She reminded me that I, as a preacher speaking before a great many people, was dealing with the gospel, the most precious thing in the world. She asked me if I thought Jesus used good grammar.

"Of course He did," I replied.

She said, "Aren't you a Jesus man, a man of the Bible?" When I nodded, she said, "Then why not follow Him in all aspects of life?"

That really got me. In a short while her compliments on my good grammar were music to my ears. When I became the founder and president of Oral Roberts University, a fully accredited university from the bachelor's degree to the doctorates, I realized how important it is to learn to speak good grammar, and do it!

We took the time to teach good grammar to our children, also to teach them to "Say your words plainly!" Our children have used and do use good grammar, and each one is very articulate.

4.   How to *Receive* After I Had Planted Seed

I was so excited about teaching people the miracle of Seed-Faith and so intent on not wanting people to think I was charging for my prayers, that I actually did not personally *receive* when God sent a supply for our needs.

In the beginning I had made a vow that I would never touch the gold or the glory. Evelyn helped me to realize that when we planted our personal seeds of faith, God was sending miracle harvests to us but I would not accept them.

I finally woke up. When God sends harvests, if we are not expecting them and recognizing them as sent by God, they pass us by. Then God's Word is not working in our lives. Luke 6:38a says, "Give, and it *shall* be given unto you." That is Jesus' own promise, and He does not go back on His promises.

I saw that if I did not learn to receive, I could not be an example—or a mentor—to the people. If the minister of the gospel is not getting his needs met, he cannot lift up the people to sow and to reap (see Gal. 6:7), to give and to receive (see Phil. 4:15).

I can assure you when husband and wife practice giving and receiving, they are a happy couple and a far greater blessing to others.

5.   The Indispensable Truth That My Wife Could Meet All My Needs

I admit that was the chief question in my mind as I became serious about getting married. There was a wide difference between my desire for women *before* I was converted and *after* I received Jesus as my personal Savior and received His call to preach the gospel.

It was like the difference between daylight and dark. Before my conversion, a woman I courted was someone I had designs on, what I could get from her.

When I became a born-again believer, something miraculous took over my whole being. A woman no longer was little more than a sex object to me, but a lady in the class of my mother or my sister Jewel.

This change was so profound it surprised me. I could date a girl without the slightest desire to lead her astray.

When I dated Evelyn, I was so unlike the other young men she had dated that it changed her entire attitude toward men. I made no pass at her.

She told me after we were married, "I felt so safe with you. I did not have to have my defenses up every minute. I could relax and express my love for you as the one I wanted to marry, the only one I had had the desire to marry."

As Evelyn and I met that weekend in Texas where she was teaching school (described in Chapter 10), I knew that I knew God had brought us together and she was the one for me. She told me I was the one for her. We were so comfortable with each other.

The Lord put it in her heart to say to me, "Oral, I want to tell you something very serious about me and our times together after we marry. It's this: I pledge to you I will meet all your needs that a wife is supposed to meet. There never will be any reason for you to be tempted by another woman or to doubt my loyalty or to feel any needs you have will not be met. The Lord has dealt with me on the responsibility and opportunity of a

Bible wife for her husband. I hope you will believe me and will be at peace about it."

I looked into her eyes and saw purity, substance as a woman, and sincerity in her face. It was one of the sweetest moments of my life, one that would expand into all the years ahead that the Lord was giving me a wife of His choice and all of my needs as a husband would be met.

I told her, "Evelyn, we will never forget this day. We know God has brought us together when we couldn't have done it ourselves. I receive your pledge as from the Lord, and I pledge to you by His help I will be faithful to you the rest of our lives together."

Neither of us could keep the tears back. It was more than a deep, emotional moment; it was two Christians marrying in the Lord.

Now, 69 years later, with 4 children, 13 grandchildren, and several great-grandchildren, I remember Evelyn's pledge. I can honestly say she has been a wife beyond compare, living up to Solomon's description of a Bible wife in Proverbs 31:10-31:

> Who can find a virtuous woman? for her price is far above rubies. The heart of her husband doth safely trust in her, so that he shall have no need of spoil. She will do him good and not evil all the days of her life. She seeketh wool, and flax, and worketh willingly with her hands. She is like the merchants' ships; she bringeth her food from afar. She riseth also while it is yet night, and giveth meat to her household, and a portion to her maidens. She considereth a field, and buyeth it: with the fruit of her hands she planteth a vineyard. She girdeth her loins with strength, and strengtheneth her arms. She perceiveth that her merchandise is

good: her candle goeth not out by night. She layeth her hands to the spindle, and her hands hold the distaff. She stretcheth out her hand to the poor; yea, she reacheth forth her hands to the needy. She is not afraid of the snow for her household: for all her household are clothed with scarlet. She maketh herself coverings of tapestry; her clothing is silk and purple. Her husband is known in the gates, when he sitteth among the elders of the land. She maketh fine linen, and selleth it; and delivereth girdles unto the merchant. Strength and honour are her clothing; and she shall rejoice in time to come. She openeth her mouth with wisdom; and in her tongue is the law of kindness. She looketh well to the ways of her household, and eateth not the bread of idleness. Her children arise up, and call her blessed; her husband also, and he praiseth her. Many daughters have done virtuously, but thou excellest them all. Favour is deceitful, and beauty is vain: but a woman that feareth the Lord, she shall be praised. Give her of the fruit of her hands; and let her own works praise her in the gates.

IMPORTANT POINTS

These are the secrets I have learned from my wife, Evelyn:

1. Put my family first.

2. It is important to control my temper.

3. Using good grammar would help me be accepted in my ministry and in any society.

4. She taught me how to receive after I had planted seed.

5. A wife can meet all her husband's needs.

24

THE FINAL WORD

If You See the Invisible, You Can Do the Impossible

As I look back over the long road I have traveled, the Holy Spirit has reminded me that without my *seeing the invisible, I could not be still doing the impossible!*

I had no specialized training, no mentors, just God's call in my heart, His Word that I absorbed day and night, and the willingness to step out by faith alone to see what God would do. Now I realize I could not have taken even the first step without first seeing the invisible. The impossible would have remained impossible.

In these pages I have tried to tell my stories of seeing the invisible and still doing the impossible. Today I look on them with awe. In many ways they all seem like a dream. But the dream is tangible, it exists, and it looks like it will last far beyond my lifetime.

I have not spared myself in revealing mistakes, blunders, and failures before I got on the right track with God. At first some religious leaders only gave me two months in the ministry, then two years. I understand why. Finally they gave up as they saw God was really doing something in what had been my pitiful life.

If there is anything in this book that suggests I am boasting, that was never in my heart. Whatever bragging I have done was meant to show that seeing the invisible means you can do the impossible if you will apply God's principles in His Word.

I have tried to write the kind of book I would have given anything for when I had a lot of trouble believing I could do the impossible.

For 54 years with every ounce of my being I have tried to keep my eyes focused on Jesus and on seeing the people as He did. I have aimed all my efforts toward bringing God's deliverance to them in spirit, mind, body, finances, family salvation, and to educating their young people. Also I have had only one desire, which is to obey God—not man or religious institutions that are not focused on being like Jesus.

This has gotten me into all kinds of controversies, held me up to ridicule by the news media, and caused satan to send persecution almost more than I could bear. In my very first year when all these things were happening, I let it get to me entirely too much. I finally got straightened out in my reaction to all negative actions. I knew I was following the Word of God and Jesus' call on my life and that He kept His anointing powerfully on me. I was keenly aware of this, and I clung to it with all my faith.

I finally learned that the only way to grow stronger is to be opposed, to have a powerful force to overcome, and at the same time to keep your composure, your temper, a good spirit, a strong outlook on life, and appreciation for your calling.

I did not grow stronger by facing weak forces, but powerful ones. Because I have stood my ground, refused to strike back, obeyed God, and stayed little in my own eyes—

I have survived!

I have kept my ministry on course.

I have seen the invisible and done the impossible...and am still doing it.

Without opposition and learning to keep it in perspective with Jesus and the Word of God, I would have fallen by the wayside the first year of my ministry.

I say, to God be all the glory.

I have learned that, if I have obeyed God according to all I understood, I could not be stopped or defeated by enemies or friends who simply misunderstood my motives.

No matter how hard I have tried, I have never reached perfection. I continue to make mistakes and have many shortcomings. What has kept me going with a substantial measure of success is following God's Word as given in Isaiah 1:19, "If ye be willing and obedient, ye shall eat the good of the land."

I believe it all comes to how you obey God's personal calling on your life, and how you commit to use your faith to its very limits. You can believe for the worst or you can release your faith to acquire the absolute best for God.

I have found it so.

I see leaders doing it wherever I minister across America. I am most impressed that many of them are from 25 to 50 years of age. Most of these successful leaders started with a handful of people, sometimes only the members of their personal family. But they, like Moses, "saw the invisible," and they went forth and "did the impossible." (See Hebrews 11:27.)

When Billy Joe Daugherty and his wife Sharon graduated from Oral Roberts University in the late 1970s, they started out in the ministry at point zero. They did not whine or cry,

"Why doesn't somebody help us? Where will we get the money? How will we get started?"

They started little, got some results, which attracted others. Now, nearly 25 years later, eight thousand attend Victory Christian Center in Tulsa every Sunday morning. Victory Christian School, K through 12, is the largest in Oklahoma, with over twelve hundred enrolled. Their Victory Bible Institute is overflowing. They have planted a score of churches and Christian schools in Russia and 12 other nations.

They saw the invisible, and they are doing the impossible. I could name a hundred just like them who began at zero and are now a dominant ministry in their area.

Creflo Dollar started World Changers Church in Atlanta less than 15 years ago. He also started at point zero. He went for excellence, refusing to compromise. Today his church seats ten thousand and is too small. The television program of his services of preaching, teaching, and healing attract millions of viewers. I preached at his church three different times and each time I returned, a greater move for God was either on the drawing boards or already launched.

When Kenneth and Gloria Copeland, with their little children, came to ORU in 1967, they wanted not only an education but also to learn to hear God's voice and to know Jesus intimately so their ministry would develop and their faith would touch the world.

As Kenneth said, "I'm the oldest freshman at Oral Roberts University," I replied, "Ken, it's never too late if you feel God called you here." He said, "Well, He's done that. When my family and I drove through the entrance with its flags of the nations representing where the students come from, my oldest daughter Terri said, 'Dad, look at the flags. We'll be with the whole world here!' We knew we were at the right place!"

When we learned Ken was an experienced commercial pilot, Bob DeWeese, my crusade manager and captain of our ministry plane, hired him to be his copilot for the weekend crusades I was conducting at that time.

He also appointed Ken to be our driver in the crusades and to serve in the invalid tent or auditorium area by helping those too sick to enter the public healing line. He would help get them ready for me to pray over them. I always prayed for these people before I prayed for those who were in the line in front of the platform.

Ken listened to my sermon, and while I was leading souls to Christ before praying for the sick, he quickly interpreted its main points to the invalids who were unable to hear the sermon, hoping to help get them better ready to receive my healing prayer.

So Ken obtained not only his education, but his introduction to my ministry, as it really is. He and Gloria stayed as long in ORU as they could before the fire of the Lord in their spirits drew them to launch their own ministry.

Today the Copeland ministry is one of the most organized and strongest worldwide ministries of deliverance on earth. It continues to grow in its powerful impact upon millions through daily television, millions of tapes and pieces of literature, and personal crusades.

There are hundreds and hundreds of others, such as Ron Luce of Teen Mania, Myles Munroe, and not least, our own son Richard and Lindsay, our precious daughter-in-law. Richard is the second president of ORU. He and Lindsay host nightly *The Hour of Healing* program on more than two hundred television stations and cable systems. The word of knowledge works mightily through them. Thousands are being healed, many of them phoning in LIFE to the program with their healing testimonies, giving hope to the same type of sick and afflicted people that my ministry did for all the years I was on the field worldwide. How proud I am of them!

In this hour, Benny Hinn, my very close friend and brother in the ministry of the anointing and God's healing power, not yet fifty years old, has a calling that is fitting the needs of hundreds of thousands of people hungry for God worldwide.

A man born in Israel, of Armenian and Greek parents, Benny immigrated as a boy with his family to Canada, and there found Jesus as His Savior and Lord. Called to preach at 21, he was greatly moved and influenced by the inimitable Kathryn Kuhlman, God's special handmaiden for many years to this nation.

Some fifteen years ago God set him apart with a unique ministry of the anointing, and since then the largest auditoriums and stadiums of the world cannot accommodate the crowds of hungry people who want the anointing and through the anointing to receive their healing.

No one in preaching, teaching, and healing, to my knowledge, has such sustained crowds—and as often.

I feel honored to have had a part in Benny's development, sharing at his request my experiences in the healing ministry as one of the pioneers of the charismatic ministry. We are very close. I believe in him, affirm him, and thrill at God's anointing on him that flows through him to multitudes of people, including kings, prime ministers, and parliaments. He is a phenomenon for God.

Benny says an even greater revival of the anointing for God's people is coming and that we are very near it. I know of no spiritual leader, especially one with such limited background, who is having such a powerful effect upon millions today, both in person and on his television program, "This Is Your Day."

The daughter of Benny and Suzanne, the other half of Benny's ministry is studying at Oral Roberts University along with over five thousand others. Benny often ministers to our entire University family and serves as a member of the ORU Board of Regents. Although not a graduate of ORU, he is much a part of the ORU outreach.

I only wish I had space to tell of all the others: including the thousands of ORU graduates in ministry, business, communications, medicine, dentistry, law, education, etc. Each makes an impact for Christ "in every man's world." But God knows, and the area where they labor knows—and I know. I cannot describe the thrill, the joy it gives me to see the successors who are going beyond my own labors for the Lord.

At one time I had no such thoughts or visions of what my ministry could do, not until I saw that God is a God of excellence. I saw that by wholehearted but simple obedience to Him, I could do everything I was called to do with excellence.

Strangely, everything I have attempted without excellence never got off the ground. I am convinced faith rolls on the wheels of excellence only.

Yes, it *can* be done. And you are the one who can do it.

Maybe for some reason you think you have not seen the invisible and feel that doing the impossible is not a real possibility. You may be discouraged or caught up in the bureaucracy of a denomination.

Yes, I think about you and pray for you. I know that lonely and often fruitless ministry. I know the doubts, the sleepless nights, the unanswerable questions from others. I know, however, the Lord is real. We can "see" Him, knowing He is not physically present in time and space but is more real than when He walked the dusty streets of Israel, preaching, teaching, and healing. He is calling us to "see Him," to "hear Him," to believe we can make personal contact with Him and He with us.

God may speak to you in a completely different way than He spoke to me. I heard Him audibly; you may or may not. You may hear Him by a deep impression in your spirit which lingers and will not go away.

We are all different and have different personalities. God speaks to us according to our personalities and in a way He knows we will understand. He does not speak to everybody audibly, but do not discount that He will speak to you in your spirit one way or the other, each equally important.

And when He *does* speak to our spirit—talk about joy, zest, enthusiasm, power, authority, and the anointing causing us to break out of our cocoons!

Yes, you *can* do it!

If a former stuttering, tuberculosis-ridden young Indian boy in an obscure county in Oklahoma can see the invisible and do the impossible—and still do it—so can you!

25

"THE FOURTH MAN"

My Sermon That Has Had the Greatest Impact on People for 54 Years

The Book of Daniel, chapter 3, contains a fantastic story:

There are certain Jews whom thou hast set over the affairs of the province of Babylon, Shadrach, Meshach, and Abednego; these men, O king, have not regarded thee: they serve not thy gods, nor worship the golden image which thou hast set up. Then Nebuchadnezzar in his rage and fury commanded to bring Shadrach, Meshach, and Abednego. Then they brought these men before the king. Nebuchadnezzar spake and said unto them, Is it true, O Shadrach, Meshach, and Abednego, do not ye serve my gods, nor worship the golden image which I have set up? Now if ye be ready that at what time ye hear the sound of the cornet, flute, harp, sackbut, psaltery, and dulcimer, and all kinds of music, ye fall down and worship the image which I have made; well: but if ye worship not, ye shall

251

be cast the same hour into the midst of a burning fiery furnace; and who is that God that shall deliver you out of my hands? Shadrach, Meshach, and Abednego, answered and said to the king, O Nebuchadnezzar, we are not careful to answer thee in this matter. [They said that because they already had their minds made up.] *If it be so, our God whom we serve is able to deliver us from the burning fiery furnace, and He will deliver us out of thine hand, O king. But if not, be it known unto thee, O king, that we will not serve thy gods, nor worship the golden image which thou hast set up.*

Then was Nebuchadnezzar full of fury, and the form of his visage [or face] *was changed against Shadrach, Meshach, and Abednego: therefore he spake, and commanded that they should heat the furnace one seven times more than it was wont to be heated. And he commanded the most mighty men that were in his army to bind Shadrach, Meshach, and Abednego, and to cast them into the burning fiery furnace. Then these men were bound in their coats, their hosen, and their hats, and their other garments, and were cast into the midst of the burning fiery furnace. Therefore because the king's commandment was urgent, and the furnace exceeding hot, the flame of the fire slew those men that took up Shadrach, Meshach, and Abednego. And these three men, Shadrach, Meshach, and Abednego, fell down bound into the midst of the burning fiery furnace. Then Nebuchadnezzar the king was astonied, and rose up in haste, and spake, and said unto his counsellors, Did not we cast three men bound into the midst of the fire? They answered and said unto the king, True, O king. He answered and said, Lo, I see four men loose, walking in the midst of the fire, and they have no hurt; and the form of the fourth is like the Son of God. Then Nebuchadnezzar came near to the mouth of the burning fiery furnace, and spake, and said, Shadrach, Meshach, and Abednego, ye servants of the most high God, come forth, and come hither. Then Shadrach, Meshach, and Abednego, came forth of the midst of the fire. And the princes, governors, and captains, and the king's counsellors, being gathered together, saw these men, upon whose bodies the fire had no power, nor was an hair of their head singed, neither were their coats changed, nor the smell of fire had passed on them.*

Then Nebuchadnezzar spake, and said, Blessed be the God of Shadrach, Meshach, and Abednego, who hath sent His angel, and delivered His servants that trusted in Him, and have changed the king's word, and yielded their bodies, that they might not serve nor worship any god, except their own God. Therefore I make a decree, That every people, nation, and language, which speak any thing amiss against the God of Shadrach, Meshach, and Abednego, shall be cut in pieces, and their houses shall be made a dunghill: because there is no other God that can deliver after this sort. Then the king promoted Shadrach, Meshach, and Abednego, in the province of Babylon (Daniel 3:12-30).

My message is entitled "The Fourth Man."

Like a diamond on a velvet couch, the city of Jerusalem sits in the geographical center of the earth. It is the city of God the great King. Here His prophets walked the streets and gave their prophecies. Here God's law went out to the ends of the earth. Here people worshiped the true God.

Far away from Jerusalem was another city, Babylon. The world still talks about Babylon. The Book of Revelation tells how it will be rebuilt. In the Battle of Armageddon, in the last days, Babylon will be restored and will play a major part when Christ comes a second time to destroy the kingdom of the devil and set up His Kingdom upon this earth.

Here lived Nebuchadnezzar, the proudest king that ever ruled an earthly throne. He had established a kingdom that had conquered the nations of the world, and he had brought back the leaders of those nations and settled them in the city of Babylon.

He had also brought their gods that they had made with their hands and worshiped. Because he saw that those gods had no power to deliver those who trusted in them, he declared himself to be god. He had his smelters make an image of himself of pure gold, a hundred feet high, and placed it in a conspicuous place in Babylon.

Any time that he wanted to, he had music played and at that sound everyone was to bow and to chant, "Great is Nebuchadnezzar our god. Great is Nebuchadnezzar our god."

There was one nation he had not conquered—Israel, with the city of Jerusalem as its capital. Nebuchadnezzar took his proud army, marched across the hot shimmering sands of the deserts, and besieged the city of God. As long as the people worshiped God and obeyed Him, they had been unconquerable—the greatest city in the world, the richest city in the world. Because the people of Israel at that time had backslidden; had turned away from God; had stopped their tithing, and therefore stopped the blessing of God coming upon them; and had turned to man-made gods; they had no will or power to resist.

With his battering rams Nebuchadnezzar tore down the walls of Jerusalem and entered, burned, and sacked the temple, which Solomon had built. He burned and sacked the city and took captive the leaders, the young and the old, the flower of the nation, as trophies of his victory.

I want you to see three young men especially: Shadrach, Meshach, and Abednego. Daniel was also in the midst. See them as they stand on one of the hills overlooking the city of Jerusalem. Hear their melancholy words as they see their city in ruins and the smoke going toward Heaven, "O Jerusalem, O Jerusalem, if we forget thee, let our right hand forget its cunning and let our tongue cleave to the roof of our mouth" (see Ps. 137:5-6).

See them again as they're ushered inside the city of Babylon, captives of the cruelest man who ever sat on a human throne. See them a few days later—hearing all kinds of music and seeing the people bow before that shining image of gold— standing on their feet, refusing to bow.

Day after day they refused to bow, until they were reported to the king, who sent for them and said, "Shadrach, Meshach, and Abednego, I've heard that you would not bow to my god. Well, I'm going to tell you that whatever God you've been serving was not able to cause your people to survive. Your cities are in ruins. You're my captives.

"And when you hear the sound of music, you bow and you give me glory. If you do not, I will cast you alive in that same hour into the midst of a burning fiery furnace. And who is that God that shall deliver you out of my hands?" These three young men came face-to-face with some of the inescapable facts of life.

First, *true faith in God will be tried.* There is a devil. There is an enemy at the gate. He comes against God's people, particularly when they become disobedient. He has more power than Nebuchadnezzar had.

These young men heard the king say, "You will bow or you will burn." Standing there, they were face-to-face with death. Their faith, which had never been tried to that extent, now was on trial. In Jerusalem there had been no such enemy. There will be a place, a time, a situation in your life and mine when we'll be tried, when the faith we have in God, the songs we sing about His reality, the declaration of our faith and our love and our commitment to Him, will be tested.

Many people don't understand that. My wife's sister, who was once under persecution for her Christian faith, said to me, "Oral, why, when we give ourselves to God, do these persecutions come? It looks like everyone should be happy that we're trying to make a better world."

I said, "Because there is a devil in the world, and he's coming against you." And she said, "Well, I wish he wouldn't." I said, "But he will." Your faith will be tried.

Let me tell you, any old dead fish can float downstream, but it takes a live one to swim upstream. If your faith is not anchored in the Son of God, if your commitment is not made, if your obedience is not established, even though you may fail now and then—when the trial of faith comes, it will pull you down. And like a dead fish, you'll be floating down through life, rather than being a live child of God, fighting against the current and building your character and establishing your witness and being a joy of the Lord to the world. It comes to every one of us.

Second, *you will encounter the two facts of life: the fact of faith, on the one hand, and the fact of compromise on the other.*

Every day of your life, everywhere you live or work or are, you will be called upon either to exercise your faith in God or to compromise the Bible, the Church, Heaven, the birth of Jesus, the cross, the resurrection, the in-filling of the Holy Spirit, the living of the Christian life, the signs and wonders, the miracles that God has for each of us. You will be tempted to compromise, but God will be there to give you strength and help for your faith to hold steady so that you don't compromise.

Nebuchadnezzar said, "I am going to give you one more chance. When you hear the sound of music if you fall down and begin to chant my name and call me God, it will be fine with you. But if you do not, I will cast you alive in the same hour into the midst of a burning fiery furnace. And who is that God that shall deliver you out of my hands?"

These three young men stood there facing faith in God on the one hand, compromise on the other hand. Your test may not be exactly like theirs, but you will be approached. Something will come up, and you will be facing the exercising of your faith, your convictions for God, or you will be tempted to compromise and let down in order to get by that persecution, that tribulation, that opposition. Someone will tell you, "If you don't bow, if you don't compromise, you will lose. You will never make it. You will never be anybody in this world. You will be sneered at, looked down on. You will never amount to anything." That's what the world says.

But God has another way called faith. Throughout the Bible you will find this statement from God, "The just shall live by faith."

You live by faith or you die by doubt. You stand up with your faith or you fall with compromise. There's nothing between the two to connect them. You go all out for faith or you go all out for compromise.

The devil is after you every day of your life. But on the other hand, the power of God is overshadowing you. The

Church is here to help establish you in the faith. The Word of God you hear builds your faith, teaches you the Word of God. The Bible that you have in your hands and the Bible you give each child and the time you spend with your children, with the Word of God, all these things are there to strengthen you. God is your friend. God is a good God. God is there to strengthen you. God is there to encourage you.

You may flip on the television, and there will be a word from some minister of the gospel or someone else who has the right word for you at that time. A neighbor may give the right word. Something in the Bible will leap out to you, like Third John 2 did to Evelyn and me 54 years ago: "Beloved, I wish above all things that thou mayest prosper and be in health, even as thy soul prospereth."

That changed our lives. That strengthened us. That showed us that if we believed that God is a good God, if we trusted Him and held on to our faith and refused to compromise, God would lift us to the highest dimensions of His supply for our needs in every area of our lives.

In a tiny little church, poverty stricken, barely making my way through the university, obscure in the world, nobody believing we'd ever amount to anything, God knew us and knew where we were and knew our address. He knew our names. He knew that someday I would be preaching to thousands and hundreds of thousands and millions of people. He knew I would be the first man in America, in the early 1950s, to be on nationwide television every week, bringing the healing line into the front rooms of the homes of America. He knew I would build a major university, Oral Roberts University in Tulsa, Oklahoma, the largest private university in Oklahoma, with bachelors', masters', and doctors' degrees. Thirty-eight years ago we were the smallest college in the state. Now we are the biggest private university in the state.

You look at yourself and you think that you are nobody or you are obscure, that people don't think about you. But God in Heaven knows your address. He knows your name. He knows your future, and He's calling out to you, "Hold on to your faith. Don't compromise. Don't compromise."

I want to call your attention to at least one of the ways we're most tempted to compromise.

We're tempted to compromise our families. That is to say, we come to Christ, we are saved, we love Him and love the Church. But if we're not careful, we may put the Church before we put our family, and we may neglect our children and not teach them the Word of God. We may see them grow up despising the Church and we may lose control over them.

My parents almost lost control over me. At near 16 years of age I ran away from home. My father was a preacher, and he loved God and he loved me and my brothers and sisters. But I couldn't see any future. I didn't want to be a preacher like my father was. I didn't want to be poor like that. I didn't want to be sneered at like that.

I really wanted to become a lawyer. I wanted to be governor of Oklahoma someday. I dreamed dreams like little children dream. And I saw no future.

I ran away, and was gone for a year, until tuberculosis struck my body. My mother is Cherokee, and tuberculosis strikes the Native American people throughout America. It killed her daddy and her two older sisters and it had settled on my body.

I was a ballplayer, and my coach brought me home. I'd fallen to the floor in a district tournament, a decisive game for the state tournament. He brought me—six feet, one and a half inches tall, 165 pounds—home, and said to my father, "I brought your son home. He's very sick."

They laid me on the bed and I didn't get up for five months. I was hemorrhaging my life away, until at the last moment the three doctors waiting on me told Reverend Roberts, "It's a matter of days now. He will be gone." My father knelt at the foot of my bed and prayed, "God, I can't stand to see my son lose his soul when he dies."

When I looked at my father's face, as the tears were streaming down, it vanished. In a moment there appeared the countenance of Jesus, and it broke me up. I saw the invisible, and I heard myself cry out, "O God, save me. Save my soul. Don't let me die like this."

The Lord came into my heart, and I leaped up from the bed. I hadn't had the strength to walk. But I leaped up in the bed and began to rejoice. I had seen the invisible, and now I was going to do the impossible.

I began the healing ministry 54 years ago, after Evelyn and I discovered Third John 2, and a farmer came to our house with his seed money of $400. He said it was not just money but a seed, and we began to study the Bible and discovered the miracle of Seed-Faith. We began to share it with the world, but above all to live it ourselves so that everything we did became a *seed*. The tithe, the ten percent that we gave, was a seed. Our ministry was a seed. Our good deeds were seeds. We began to expect God to give back to us, which was not taught in those days.

I became so carried away with my ministry that I began to neglect our four children. I came home after 16 or 17 days away—and that was every month—and my wife stayed home and raised my children. She worked with them and did everything that she could, teaching them the Sunday school lesson on Saturday because she knew that in the little church they attended, some of the teachers would not know the lesson. Often they'd call on one of my children to stand up and teach.

When I came home, I was tired. I wanted to get some rest. I wanted to have some time. I loved my children. I hugged them. They hugged me. We had some time together, and then I began to drift away during the next ten days before I went to my next crusade. I made a terrible error. It was a compromise. I was compromising my children.

Did you know that in the Bible God established the family before He established the Church? Do you know your family should come first before your ministry does? God is first, but not our ministry. Our children, our family is first.

Evelyn said, "Oral, you're making a terrible mistake. These children may grow up and hate you as a preacher, hate the ministry." God spoke to me, "You're compromising. You're bowing."

Nebuchadnezzar said to these three young men, "You will burn or you will bow. You will bow to my god or you will burn in my furnace." The law of compromise is, you will bow or you will burn. If you compromise or if you believe God, there's going to be a difference in the results. If you hold on to your faith—Nebuchadnezzar said, "and not bow, you will burn."

But God had spoken, and in their hearts they knew if they bowed, they would burn. God said, "*If you compromise, you will lose what you compromised to get.*"

No matter what you get by compromise, you will never enjoy it. You will never keep it. It will never benefit you. Any compromise you make, little, middle-sized, or big, has sorrow and loss at the end.

But if you hold on to your faith and you go into the fiery furnace, God will see to it that if you won't bow, you won't burn. Something miraculous will happen to deliver you because your faith is your victory.

Third, *life's fiery furnaces are in the world today.* Everywhere you turn, there's somebody or something to get you to compromise. The threat is there, either said or not said, but you know it's there. "You'll lose your job, you won't be promoted, you will never have a nice home, a nice car. You will never be anybody. You will never be recognized. Life will deny you of your goals, rob you of your dreams, kill your destiny." That's what compromise says. That's what it means. That's what satan has in his mind when he comes to get you or me to compromise.

I made a major change in my life with my children. When I came home, they knew I had to have at least a day to rest and to get some of my strength back because I worked hard.

On the last day of my crusade, there would be some ten thousand sick people stand up in long lines, and I'd lay my right hand upon each and every one of them, which is almost impossible for a human being to do. So you can imagine what shape my body was in after I flew home. And I needed rest.

But I made a decision, and when I got rest, I'd take my children one by one and I'd love them and I'd teach them the Bible. God said about Abraham, "I know that Abraham will teach his children. I know he will command his children." My very presence as the daddy in that family was a command to my children. They knew how I lived, how clean my life was, how I loved God, how my ministry meant so much to me.

But suddenly I began to change and to take time. I would put the little ones on my knee and read passages in the Bible. I would tell them stories of the Bible. I would gather them together, along with Evelyn, and each of us would tell them stories of the Bible. I taught them to pray. I taught each one to say grace at the table. I would play with them, and spend quality time with them. I quit compromising.

I knew now through my wife's intervention and my decision to change and not compromise that I would have an influence on my children. And I want you to know all four children came to Christ and have lived for Christ. I want you to know all my 13 grandchildren—one of them is in Heaven—but all 12 of them are saved by God's grace.

I want you to know they are all in church. I want you to know that Roberta, one of my daughters, is an attorney. She serves the charismatic community in Tulsa, and is one of the most popular lawyers in the city. My son, Richard, is president of Oral Roberts University. I was president the first 30 years. Now he's been president nine years, and he's doing a better job than his daddy did.

I tell you, success without a successor is failure. My son is supposed to be better than his daddy was. We're supposed to raise children who will go beyond us in their faith.

You may be in a burning fiery furnace right now, because it comes in different ways. A fiery furnace to me may not be one to you. One to you may not be the same to me. But you may be in a condition right now where you're suffering, where you're under a threat, where you're about to do something that will compromise your integrity with God, that will cause your faith to weaken and the devil to get an upper hand for a temporary gain.

But God knows if you compromise, you will lose what you compromised to get. And God knows if you refuse to compromise—no matter how bleak the circumstances look and how defeat seems to loom so near you—that you may temporarily lose, but before it's over, you will not lose. God will pick you up. God will restore to you seven times what the devil stole from you.

I'm telling you, when you live by faith, you're on the winning side.

Well, the king said, "What's your verdict?" And they said, "We're not careful to answer you in this matter because our minds are already made up. We don't have to think what to say. We know what to say. We may burn in that furnace that you've heated seven times hotter, but we won't bow to your god."

There comes a time when you put your foot down and you say, "Devil, get out of my life." You put your foot down and you say, "Devil, take your hands off God's property, me."

The king didn't wait. He threw them in the furnace, and he slammed the door and waited till they were burned to a crisp. In a few minutes he had the door opened, and he looked in, and the hair on his neck stood up. He said to his counselors, "Did not we cast three men in there, all of them bound?" They said, "That's right." He said, "I see four of them. They are loose. They're walking around in the midst of the fire, and the form of the fourth one looks like the Son of God." The form of the Fourth Man in the furnace.

Who is this Fourth Man? I'll try to tell you who He is from the Books of the Bible.

In Genesis He is the Seed of the Woman.

In Exodus He's the Passover Lamb.

In Leviticus He is our High Priest.

In Numbers the Pillar of Cloud by day and the Pillar of Fire by night.

In Deuteronomy the Prophet like unto Moses.

In Joshua the Captain of our Salvation.

In Judges our Judge and Lawgiver.

In Ruth our Kinsman Redeemer.

In First and Second Samuel our Trusted Prophet.

In Kings and Chronicles our Reigning King.

In Ezra our Faithful Scribe.

In Nehemiah the Rebuilder of the Broken-Down Walls of Human Life.

In Esther our Mordecai.

In Job our Ever-Living Redeemer.

In Psalms the Lord our Shepherd.

In Proverbs and Ecclesiastes He is our Wisdom.

In the Song of Solomon the Lover and the Bridegroom.

In Isaiah the Prince of Peace.

In Jeremiah the Righteous Branch.

In Lamentations the Weeping Prophet.

In Ezekiel the wonderful Four-Faced Man.

In Daniel the Fourth Man in the burning fiery furnace.

In Hosea the Faithful Husband, forever married to the backslider.

In Joel the Baptizer with the Holy Ghost and Fire.

In Amos our Burden-Bearer.

In Obadiah the Mighty to Save.

In Jonah the great Foreign Missionary.

In Micah the Messenger of Beautiful Feet.

In Nahum the Avenger of God's Elect.

In Habakkuk God's Evangelist, crying, "Revive Thy work in the midst of the years" (Hab. 3:2).

In Zephaniah the Savior.

In Haggai the Owner of all the silver and gold in the earth.

In Zechariah the Fountain opened up in the House of David for Sin and Uncleanness.

In Malachi the Sun of Righteousness, rising with Healing in His Wings.

Who is this Fourth Man?

In Matthew He's the Messiah.

In Mark the Wonder-Worker.

In Luke the Son of Man.

In John the Son of God.

In Acts He's the Signs and Wonders of the Holy Spirit.

In Romans He is the One who makes all things work together for good to those who love God.

In First and Second Corinthians He is the Fruit of the Spirit and the Gifts of the Spirit.

In Galatians He's the Redeemer from the Curse of the Law.

In Ephesians the Christ of Unsearchable Riches.

In Philippians the God who Supplies all our Needs.

In Colossians the Fulness of the Godhead Bodily.

In First and Second Thessalonians our Soon-Coming King.

In First and Second Timothy our Mediator between God and Man.

In Titus a Faithful Pastor.

In Philemon a Friend that Sticketh Closer than a Brother.

In Hebrews the Blood of the Everlasting Covenant.

In James the Great Physician.

In First and Second Peter the Chief Shepherd, who soon shall appear with a Crown of Unfading Glory.

In First, Second and Third John He is Everlasting Love.

In Jude the Lord coming with Ten Thousands of His Saints.

In Revelation the King of kings and the Lord of lords.

Who is this Fourth Man?

He's Abel's Sacrifice.

He's Noah's Rainbow.

He's Abraham's Ram.

He's Isaac's Wells.

He's Jacob's Ladder.

He's Samuel's Horn of Oil.

He's David's Slingshot.

He's John the Baptist's Lamb of God.

He's a Father to the orphan, a Husband to the widow.

To those traveling the dark night, He's the Bright and Morning Star. To those of us who travel the lonesome valley, He's the Lily of the Valley, the Rose of Sharon, Honey in the Rock, and the Staff of Life.

Who is this Fourth Man? He's the Everlasting God.

He's the Eternal Ruler, and the government of our life is upon His shoulder.

Who is He? He is Jesus of Nazareth, the Son of the living God. And I want to tell you, I'm proud to serve Him!

Now let me give you three things to sum up this message. Number one, you're freer in the furnace than you are outside. You are freer when you live by your faith than you are by compromising and seeming to get all the stuff they promised. You're freer.

You have more freedom in your spirit. You have a more peaceful mind. You have a body that rests better. You have a courage that doesn't fail. You have friends that will stick closer than a brother. You have a church against which the devil and the gates of hell can never prevail. You have a Bible that's everlasting, in which Christ is the Way, the Truth, and the Life. So when you refuse to compromise and live by faith, you're freer. You're freer, even if they cast you into life's fiery furnaces.

Number two, you have a witness. Most Christians would like to have a witness. They'd like to have something about them that would draw others to the Lord—non-Christians as well as weak Christians.

In Revelation we're told that we overcome by the blood of the Lamb and by the word of our testimony. Here are three young men in a strange city, captives to a heathen king, who demands that they either bow or burn. They have no one to turn to but their God.

But what happens? When the king said, "Open the door of the furnace and throw them in," something happened in the spiritual realm. The Fourth Man stood up by His Father's side in Heaven, and a thrill went through Heaven. When they picked them up, the Bible says that the soldiers who bound them to throw them in got too close to the fire, and the fire burned them up. They weren't made out of the right kind of stuff.

When they were throwing them in, the Fourth Man rose from His Father's throne and, leaping into time and space and coming faster than the speed of sound or light, entered into Babylon and into that fiery furnace. They didn't know, when they threw Shadrach, Meshach, and Abednego into the flames, that they threw them into Jesus' arms. He tore off their bonds, and He spoke to the fire and He said, "You shall not singe their hair or scorch their clothes or burn their bodies." He robbed the fire of its violence.

The king said, "That fourth one looks like the Son of Man. There's no other God that can deliver after this sort." There's the witness. Here are three young men who have a witness. How do we have a Christian witness? We live by faith.

Someone said, "Oral, what is faith?" That's the question I asked God 54 years ago. "God, You tell us to believe and have faith. What is faith?" And He said this: "Faith is when your heart is supernaturally emptied of doubt and filled with a knowing that you know that you know that you know that you know. And in that moment of knowing, you can't doubt."

I said, "God, how do I get faith?" He said, "Don't you remember in Romans 12:3 where I said I have given the measure of faith to every person?" He said, "Faith is not something you get. It's something you already have. I've already given it to you."

When you release your faith to God, the Holy Spirit supernaturally empties your heart of doubt and fills you with this knowing, and you know that you know that you know. In that moment you can't doubt.

Number three, promotion is coming. The Bible says that Nebuchadnezzar promoted Shadrach, Meshach, and Abednego, and said, "If any man comes against their God, he's coming against me. For no other God can deliver after this sort." If you live by faith and refuse to compromise, God is going to promote you. He's done it for me; He'll do it for you. Just watch and see.

My soul is soaring toward God right now. I've never felt closer to God in my life. Evelyn and I have walked together 63 years. God has been with us. We have been in that fiery furnace scores and scores of times.

The controversy about my healing ministry and revealing that God is a good God and all that through the years was almost more than I could bear. But I took my stand. I want to tell you, at 84 years of age, I take my stand again today that God is my Father. Jesus is my Savior. The Holy Ghost is my Comforter. Salvation is in my soul. I am called to preach the gospel and to bring deliverance to lost and suffering humanity! I have done it, and I am doing it by God's grace!

I'm still doing the impossible, and so can you! The Fourth Man is still real, and He's here to give you the anointing, the power to do it. You're going to win because the Fourth Man goes into the fiery furnace with you—and brings you out! Amen and amen.

Additional copies of this book and other
book titles from DESTINY IMAGE are
available at your local bookstore.

For a complete list of our titles,
visit us at www.destinyimage.com
Send a request for a catalog to:

Destiny Image® Publishers, Inc.

P.O. Box 310
Shippensburg, PA 17257-0310

*"Speaking to the Purposes of God for This
Generation and for the Generations to Come"*